LEARN ENGLISH IN 21 LESSONS

Published by
Lotus Press Publishers & Distributors

LEARN ENGLISH IN 21 LESSONS

S. Shankar

Lotus PRESS

4735/22, Prakash Deep Building,
Ansari Road, Darya Ganj,
New Delhi-110002

Lotus Press Publishers & Distributors
Unit No. 220, 2nd Floor, 4735/22, Prakash Deep Building,
Ansari Road, Darya Ganj, New Delhi- 110002
Ph.: 41325510, 098118-38000
E-mail: lotuspress1984@gmail.com
www.lotuspress.co.in

Learn English in 21 Lessons

ISBN 81-8382-135-9

Printed & Published by: Lotus Press Publishers & Distributors, New Delhi-02

PREFACE

English is one of the most popularly and universally used languages in the world today. Considering the universality and wide acceptance of this language, we notice that it is spoken all around us even in our daily lives. If we turn on the television, we can see the new sreader reading out news in English. Besides, there are many foreign channels being telecast which exclusively use Englsih as the language of communication.

Even in banks, English is widely used as a medium of communication. English is the language of modern communication and the language of the Internet. The use of this language is not limited to only these spheres. There are many more like science, astronomy, finance, economy etc. Ever wondered, why so many fields of daily life use English as the medium for communication? This is because English is one of the most commonly known, understood languages. Thus, to target a larger audience or customer base, English is used in many spheres as the official and formal language.

Having understood the universality and popularity of this much-loved language, let us now try to imagine what the plight of a person who is unfamiliar with this language will be in this English-speaking world that surrounds us? You would not need to think very hard for the answer. Surely, the position of such a person will be very awkward and may even prove to be quite embarrassing at times. To avoid such awkwardness, the only way is to become familiar with this language. This is precisely what this book also aims at. The book has been so designed as to meet the day-to-day needs of those who need a compact handbook on English speaking, a guide that can help them to know precisely what they need to learn and leave out whatever is unnecessary.

The book should be helpful to those desirous of learning and improving English-speaking skills. It covers all aspects of the English language, that is pronunciation, grammar and vocabulary, so that no area pertaining to spoken English is left out. In fact, the book has been divided into four sections that cover all essential aspects. These sections are: Pronunciation Skills, Basic Grammar, Functional Grammar and Expanding Vocabulary. Effort has been made to incorporate all concepts that a person may need to use in his/her everyday life. Some advanced concepts have also been included so that in rare situations, where knowledge of a little advanced English is required, the speaker should not feel hesistant or inadequately equipped. This book aims to help a person become an expert where English speaking is concerned. Yes, that's it, you can actually learn and master English just like many other fluent speakers you see so often. The book will also assist persons who do not wish to enrol for any course in English speaking and wish to do it by means of self-study.

And, above all, it will also help those who wish to gain adequate knowledge to speak fluent English in their every day lives. Before, we plunge into the various topics and concepts, please remember that practice makes a man perfect. Unless a person practices, he/ she may lose touch or even forget whatever has been learnt. For the same reason, it will be helpful to undertake regular practice sessions after you have finished reading this book so that you do not lose touch with whatever you have so painstakingly learnt.

Author

CONTENTS

LESSON 1

History of the English Language and its Present Position

History of the English Language

English is an Anglo-Frisian or a West Germanic language. German-speaking people from northwest Germany and Jutland invaded what is now known as Eastern England around the fifth century A.D. The original language of this region was soon replaced.

The Germanic dialects gradually fused and formed what is today called Old English, which resembled some coastal dialects in the present north-west Germany and the Netherlands. Throughout the history of written Old English, it retained an artificial structure closer to that of Proto-Indo-European. Spoken Old English in the meanwhile lost its complex noun case system and started to depend heavily on prepositions and fixed word-order in order to convey its meaning. Over a period of time, North German and Celtic languages worked their influence on Old English. The period of Norman Conquest of England beginning from 1066 and contuinuing for about three centuries thereafter, saw the assimilation of several Norman words into Old English, especially those related to legal and administrative fields. Later, many words were borrowed directly from Greek and Latin, leaving a parallel vocabulary that still persists even well into modern times. The Norman influence played a part in the development of English over the following centuries, resulting in what is now known as Middle English.

During the 15th century, Middle English was transformed by the vowel swing, the spread of a standardised London-based dialect in government and administration, and the standardising effect of printing. The origins of early modern English can be traced back to the time of the famous English dramatist, William Shakespeare.

Spread of Present-Day English

In general, English is a vague collection of languages called "English" because their common origin is the national language spoken in England by the English people. This national language gradually spread over other parts of the world and its different alternate versions picked up popularity. Some such commonly used variants of the English language include American (US) English, Australian English, New Zealand English, Zimbabwe English, Trinidad English, Philippines English, Caribbean English, South Africa English and Canada English, etc.

Apart from these people who speak English as their first or primary language, there are also many others in other countries of the world, whose native language is a non-English variant, but who speak and know English as a second and a foreign language. In different countries and cultures, English has different positions. There are countries where English is the native language and then there are countries where English is a widely known second language and there are also countries where English has no special position. In the first two cases, it is necessary to know and learn English, because it forms an integral part of the day-to-day communication. In the third case, importance of English is evident from the fact that it is required for promoting international relations and fostering finance and business with other countries of the world. Thus, we observe how important it is to know and learn English, irrespective of the part of the world that we may belong to. This language forms an important part and parcel of our social and commercial lives and we would with feel handicapped and isolated unless we are familiar and fluent in the language.

Varieties of English

- *Basic English* is a simplified form for easy international usage. It is used by international businesses to write manuals and communicate.
- *Special English* is a simple version of English used by the Voice of America, the official radio and broadcasting system of the US government. It uses a vocabulary of only 1500 words.
- *English Spelling Reform* is a collective term used for all campaigns to simplify spellings in English language and make it simple and rationally consistent.
- *English as lingua-franca for Europe or Euro-English* is a concept that aims to standardise the use of English language in the European Union. This iniative attempts to standardise English vocabulary, grammar and spelling so that regional variations can be avoided that often make learning English difficult for many Europeans.
- *Seaspeak, Policespeak and Airspeak*, all based on restricted vocabularies, have been designed with a view to aid international cooperation and communication in specific areas.
- *E Prime* is an altered English vocabulary that excludes the verb "to be." Its supporters believe that this language compels its speakers and listeners to think differently. They feel that such a language is easily read by a majority of the people.
- *Manually Coded English* consists of many systems to represent the English language with hand signs, designed primarily for use in deaf education.

The English language that we know in its present form is an amalgam of different influences, such as French, Greek, Dutch and Latin, etc. All these varied influences have worked over the history of mankind in order to pass on to us the legacy of a very rich language, English, as we know it in its present form.

Having understood the history of the English language, its features and different varieties as prevalent all across the globe, we now turn our attention towards learning to speak this global language and would endeavour to master its usages.

A Dominant International Language

English is the dominant international language in science, communications, business and finance, aviation, research, education, politics, banking, entertainment and diplomacy. The influence of the British empire was the primary reason for the initial spread of the language much beyond the British Isles. Following World War II, the growing economic and cultural influence of the United States made a momentous contribution to the spread of this language in different parts of the world.

As we are all well-aware, a practical knowledge of English is required in many fields, professions, and occupations. English is studied and spoken by almost a billion people all over the world, to at least a basic level. The pre-dominance and popularity of this language can be adjudged from the fact that English is one of the six official languages of the United Nations.

Almost 380 million people across the globe speak English as their first language. English today is probably the third largest language by the number of native speakers, following Chinese and Spanish. However, if we combine the number of native and non-native speakers of English, it is possibly the most commonly spoken language in the world.

United States, United Kingdom, New Zealand, Australia, Ireland and South Africa are some countries where English is the first languange. Some of the countries where English is spoken as a second language include India, Pakistan, Ghana, Fiji, Bangladesh, Kenya, Nambia and Sri Lanka, etc.

A Universal Language

English is such a widely spoken language that it has often been referred to as a "global language", the *lingua franca* of the modern era. Although English is not an official language in many countries, it is currently the language most often taught as a second language all across the world. It is, by international treaty, the official language for aerial and maritime communications, as well as one of the official languages of the European Union, the United Nations, and most international athletic organisations, such as the International Olympic Committee.

English is most often studied as a foreign language in the European Union, Taiwan, South Korea, Japan, China and India.

Books, magazines, and newspapers written in English are available in many countries around the world. English is also the most commonly used language in sciences.

English is used extensively in political communications. When political heads and leaders from across the world meet together to discuss or seek consensus on important issues of political importance, the fluency in English always has an added advantage and provides the user an edge over others. Agreed, translators and interpretors are also available, but a translated script can never really measure upto the original. It may lead to misunderstandings and misconstrued meanings.

Banking is another field that banks heavily on the use of this language. Often, English is used to arrive at a common undserstanding of the problem and attempt its solution, when bankers and clients belong to diffferent cultures and speak different native languages.

English is also used for writing stuff,such as research work.The prospects of a work to sell more increase potentially if it is written in English because the number of people who are fluent in and conversant with English far exceed the number of pople who may be acquainted with any partiular native language worldwide. Usually researchers all over the world know English and use it a lot, and often the relevant terminology is more stable and well-known in English than in any other native language. Thus, the selection of a English as a medium of communication increases the number of interested people who can understand a particular text.

The importance of the Internet has grown enormously in all fields of human life. Now, it is imperative to know how to use Internet services and, as an extension of this, also know how to read and write English. One may feel isolated on the Internet if the person is not familiar with English.

This language is also popularly used in education, both primary as well as higher education. English is used as a medium by teachers to communicate with students. The growing significance of English all over the world necessitates the need for the future generation also to acquire fluency in this languange. The use of English is by no means restricted to these fields only. Some other fields where this language is used commonly include international finance, business and commerce etc.

Have you ever wondered, how English has acquired this universal position? In order to obtain an answer to this question, it is necessary to see how the language evolved over time and finally came to occupy the centrestage where it stands today.

How has English Acquired this Universal Position?

If we look back, we notice that there have been many more or less universal languages, such as Latin and Greek in the Roman empire, medieval Latin in Western Europe, followed later by French and English. Of all these languages, no language has been really universal or global, in the real sense of the term. But the current position held and enjoyed by English comes closest to the definition of an internationally-accepted and popularly used language.

The rise of imperialism and colonialism may be seen as the main factor responsible for the universal position occupied by English language today. Imperialism refers to the conquest of a large area of a nation by another nation. The occupier is referred to as the "coloniser" and the occupied as the "colonised". This process following the political acquistion, followed a cultural integration and led to the formation of an empire. Usually the language of the conquerer also became the language of the conquered state, at times almost wiping out the original languages of the conquered areas.

Gradually, with time, the imperialist dominations died a natural death all over the world. Even though the colonisers left the occupied states, the cultural values inculcated by them, including the use of a foreign language remained indelible.

As regards to the English language, it would have remained as a national language of the England, had it not so happened that the English first conquered the rest of the British Isles, then many other parts of the world. Gradually, some English colonies in various parts of the world started rebelling against the imperialist rule and set up their own independent states. In many of these countries, later on, different variants of English language came to be used. And thus,with all these variations, the universality of this language became all the more colourful and complete.

■

PART I

PRONUNCIATION SKILLS

Need for Enhancing Pronunciation Skills

Everyone is desirous of speaking English fluently, just like any native English speaker, but correct English pronunciation is often a major hurdle for many people.

If we look around us, we notice that some people are able to express themselves very well, whereas some others feel shy, timid and unwilling to talk or participate in a discussion because the latter feel scared at the prospect of committing any blunder that may make them a laughing stock. Needless to mention, the lack of confidence of such people is clearly evident.

In order to understand pronunciation skills, it is important to distinguish between a good and a bad or poor pronunciation. A poor English pronunciation may end up confusing the listener, even though the speaker may have used advanced English grammar. On the other extreme, good English pronunciation will make people understand our language easily and they would be more willing to listen to us.

So, it's all in an accurate pronunciation of words and the sentences that join such words.

A perfect pronunciation of English definitely scores over the usage of complex words and even a strong accent. There is no point in using complex words with an acquired accent, when our pronunciation is bad, because a bad pronunciation is enough to put off any intelligent listener, even without waiting for the accent and the intricate words to flow.

Hence, we see how an accurate pronunciation is indispensable to flawless and perfect English. This is the main reason why English teachers all over the world attach a lot of significance to correct pronunciation.

■

LESSON 2

Conversational Skills

Have you ever wondered what distinguishes a good English speaker from an average or a poor speaker? It is the conversational skills of the person. Good conversational skills are the essence of good pronunciation. A speaker of good English will be able to pronounce different words and sounds of the language accurately. He/She will be fluent in the spoken language and be able to speak without committing any embarrassing grammatical errors. He/She will also have an accent that is easy to understand and at the same time appears pleasant to hear.

Hence, we notice that in order to improve our conversational skills, we need to work on our pronunciation skills and attempt to acquire a pleasant accent and fluency in our spoken language.

Pronunciation

Levels of English Pronunciation

There are three levels of English pronunciation:

- *Level 1:* People often do not understand what we want to say. We, invariably, use the wrong sounds in English words.
- *Level 2*: People understand what we say, but find it unpleasant to listen to us.
- *Level 3*: People understand what we say and find our English pleasant to listen to.
- Level 1 will be referred to as poor and bad pronunciation,

where we use the wrong sounds and people are unable to comprehend what we are saying.

- Level 2 is an intermediate level between bad and good communication. If placed at this level, people are able to understand what we say but find listening to us unpleasant and distasteful.
- Level 3 is a level that may be described as good pronunciation. Our language is perfectly understandable and at the time pleasant to hear.

Apart from pronunciation problems, some other hurdles that poor or average speakers often face are difficulties in coping with fluency and accent of the language. Let us look at these in a little more detail.

Fluency

Fluency is very important in speaking good English. But if the fluent conversation is full of grammatical errors, the speaker may not be able to get his/her ideas across easily and clearly. Thus, while focusing on fluent speaking, it is also important to avoid grammatical errors because even a fluent speaker may appear awkward and feel embarrassed if his/her speech is full of grammatical mistakes.

Accent

It is very important to understand that good pronunciation is not a perfect American or a flawless British accent. English is one of the most spoken languages in the world and is spoken differently in different parts. The accent of American English is very different from British or Canadian English. So, it really does not matter if we also have our own individual accent.

But having said that, what we must remember is that the English language, which we speak, must be close and near to the standards of American or British English. This implies that we often come across people from different countries who speak English with an accent of their respective country. For example, a resident of France will speak English with a French accent, while an Indian on the other hand will adopt an Indian accent while speaking English.

A good accent is one that is easy to understand and at the same time pleasant to hear. The rule is: If we are close to the standard (of either American or British English), we can always communicate with ease and our English will appear pleasant to the listener. On the other hand, if we are distanced from the standard, often we may find it difficult to communicate successfully.

We, therefore, notice that accurate pronunciation, fluency without any grammatical errors and an accent close to the standards of acceptable English, are essential in order to acquire good conversational skills in English. If you are keen on improving your conversation skills and wish to become proficient, it is necessary to focus on these areas.

Further in this section, we shall try to unfold some simple ways to improve English conversational skills. We would attempt to understand the phonological components such as syllable, stress, phonemes and phonetics, knowledge of which is essential in order to master the art of perfect English vocabulary.

■

LESSON 3

Understanding Syllable, Stress and Rhythm

Syllable, stress and rhythm are important components of good pronunciation. Understanding what syllables to stress in words and what words to stress in a sentence is important as it is indispensable to help you communicate effectively with native and fluent speakers of English language. Maintaining the rhythm of the language is also very important as it helps the speaker to sound fluent and natural.

Although it is important to know a little about these parts of pronunciation, these are best mastered only with regular practice.

Let us now look at each of these in some detail.

Syllable

Syllable is a unit of organisation for a succession of speech sounds. Syllables are considered to be phonological building blocks of words. They are very important because they influence the rhythm of a language, its prosody and stress patterns, etc.

A syllable consists of three parts: onset, nucleus and coda. Onset is the initial or the first part of a syllable, nucleus is the central part and coda is the concluding part. Nucleus in most cases is a vowel. Onset and coda are often consonant/s or consonant clusters. Though a syllable may or may not contain onset or coda, it will definitely contain a nucleus.

Words may be classified into three kinds, depending on the number of syllables that they contain. A word that consists of one syllable is called monosyllabic. One that contains two syllables is called disyllabic. Trisyllabic is a word that consists of three syllables and a word that contains more than three syllables is called polysyllabic.

Thus, we notice that each word contains syllables. But, the number of syllables in a word may be one, two, three or more. Now, let's look at some words and see how many syllables they contain:

Word	No. Of Syllables	Type Of Word
Cat	1	Monosyllabic
Bird	1	Monosyllabic
Quiet (Qui-et)	2	Disyllabic
Monkey (Mon-key)	2	Disyllabic
Indigent (In-di-gent)	3	Trisyllabic
Indulgent (In-dul-gent)	3	Trisyllabic
Intelligence (In-telli-gen-ce)	4	Polysyllabic
Unrealistic (Un-re-a-lis-tic)	5	Polysyllabic

We notice that almost every syllable contains at least one vowel or vowel sound.

Stress

In linguistics, stress may be defined as the relative emphasis that may be given to certain syllables in a word. English is often referred to as a stress-timed language. In terms of a layman, stress may be understood as the extra energy or force with which we sometimes articulate certain words. This means that stress in a spoken sentence occurs at regular intervals and the length it takes you to say a particular word or sentence depends on the number of stressed syllables contained in that word or sentence, rather than the number of syllables itself.

In English language, some syllables are stressed, which we speak with a certain emphasis. Some others that are simply glided over are known as non-stressed syllables. The same syllable in different words can be used as stressed or non-stressed. The stressed syllables appear at a steady rate in English language and the non-stressed syllables are abridged to contain them.

Some other languages, such as, French or Italian are syllabic languages in which each syllable receives equal importance. This does not however mean that there is no stress. Stress is definitely there but each syllable has its own length.

English pronunciation focuses on specific stressed words while quickly gliding over the other, non-stressed, words. Proper stressing of the right words is indispensable to good pronunciation.

Stressed words are considered **content words:** These are:

Nouns:	donkey, finger.
Most Principal Verbs:	exit, recruit.
Adjectives:	average, interesting.
Adverbs:	often, carefully.

Non-stressed words are considered **function words:** These include:

Determiners:	a, an, the.
Auxiliary verbs:	am, were, don't, can.
Prepositions:	like, before, of, next to, opposite.
Conjunctions:	and, but, while, as.
Pronouns:	they, he, she.

Exceptions

The above rules are applicable to what is called 'neutral' or normal stress. But sometimes we can stress a word that would normally be only a structure word. Let us understand this with the help of an example:

"He has been to France, hasn't he?"

"No, HE hasn't, but SHE has."

In this case, HE and SHE, which are ordinarily non-stressed words, are stressed in order to provide correct information and to correct the speaker. Note also that when 'be' is used as a main verb, it is usually unstressed (even though in this case it is a content word).

While learning English pronunciation, you must remember that non-stressed words and syllables are often "swallowed" or "gulped down" in English. Always focus on pronouncing stressed words well, non-stressed words can be glided over. Do not focus on pronouncing each word because this can often result in faulty and incorrect pronunciation. Focus only on the stressed words in each sentence.

Thus, we notice that in English language, there is word stress, where certain syllables of a word are stressed and there is sentence stress, where certain words contained in a sentence are stressed.

Word Stress

Word stress is the key to understanding spoken English. Native speakers of English use word stress naturally. Word stress is so natural for them that they do not even know when they use it. Non-native speakers who speak English to native speakers without using word stress often find it difficult to understand native speakers, especially those speaking fast.

All words of more than one syllable have word stress. This means that at least one of the syllables is l o n g e r and **louder** than the other syllables.

In the following examples, stressed syllables are in capital letters:

Column A	Column B	Column C
PHOtograph	pho**TO**graphy	photo**GRA**phic
ACtivate	re**VI**talize	uni**QUE**
MULtiply	re**GI**ment	entert**AIN**

Column A contains words in which the first syllable is stressed, such as **PHO**tograph, **AC**tivate and **MUL**tiply. Column B contains words in which the middle syllable is stressed, like re**VI**talize, re**GI**ment and column C consists of words in which the last or the second last syllable is stressed. Last syllable is stressed in uni**QUE** and entert**AIN** and in photo**GRA**phic, the second last syllable is stressed.

As we can notice, in English, we do not say each syllable with the same force or strength. In one word, we emphasise one syllable. We say one syllable very loudly and the other syllables very quietly.

Let us take the words **photograph**, **photographer** and **photographic**. Do they sound the same when spoken? No. This is because one syllable in each word is accentuated or stressed and it is not always the same syllable. For example, in **photograph**, the stressed syllable is **PHO,** in **photography,** it is pho**TO**graphy and in **photographic**, it is photo**GRA**phic. As a result, each word produces a different sound.

The stressed syllables written in bold letters are strong, while those that are not stressed are 'weak' or 'small' or 'quiet'. Native speakers of English.listen for the stressed syllables, not the weak syllables. If you use word stress in your speech, you will immediately and automatically improve your pronunciation and your comprehension of spoken English.

Try to hear the stress in individual words each time you listen to English - on the radio, the television or in films. Listen carefully in order to hear and recognise it. Once this has been mastered, you can incorporate the learning into your spoken English.

There are two important rules about word stress:

One word, one stress. One word cannot have two stresses. So if you hear two stresses, you have heard two words, not one word. Two stresses cannot be one word. It is true that there can be a 'secondary' stress in some words. But a secondary stress is much smaller than the main [primary] stress, and is only used in long words.

Examples

Stress on first syllable

Rule	Most **2-syllable nouns**
Example	DONkey, PHOtograph
Rule	Most **2-syllable adjectives**
Example	HAppy, SMart

Stress on last syllable

Rule Most **2-syllable verbs**

Example To imPORT, to viSIT

The stress is always on a vowel.

Word stress is an integral part of the language, used by English speakers to communicate quickly and effectively. If, for example, you do not hear a word clearly, you can still understand the word because of the position of the stress.

Where to put word stress?

There are some rules about which syllable to stress. Though the rules are rather complicated, the best way to learn is from experience. Listen carefully to spoken English and try to develop a feeling for the 'music' of the language. When you learn a new word, you should also learn its stress pattern. A dictionary is also helpful as it provides the phonetic spellings of words and indicates which syllables to stress.

Only vowels are stressed, not consonants. Here are some more, rather complicated, rules that can help you understand where to put the stress. But do not rely on them too much, because there are many exceptions. It is better to try to 'feel' the music of the language and to add the stress naturally.

Stress on penultimate syllable. Here second last syllables are stressed.

Rule	*Example*
Words ending in **-ic**	GRAPHic, geoGRAPHic, photoGRAphic
Words ending in **-sion** and **-tion**	VIsion, reveLAtion

Stress on antepenultimate syllable. Here third last syllables are stressed.

Rule	*Example*
Words ending in **-cy**, **-ty**, **-phy** and **-gy**	deMOcracy, dependaBIlity, phoTOgraphy.
Words ending in **-al**	CRItical, LOgical

Compound words. These are words with two parts.

Rule	*Example*
For compound **nouns**, the stress is on the **first** part	BLUEbird, DININGtable, BOOKshop
For compound **adjectives**, the stress is on the **second** part	bad-TEMpered, ill-MANnered
For compound **verbs**, the stress is on the **second** part	to underESTIMATE, to overLOOK

Noun+Noun Compounds (2-word compound nouns). Similar to the rule for compound nouns, the first part of the compound—here, the first word gets the stress.

Air conditioner

Book store

Ham burger

French fry

Cashier's counter

Lawyer's office

Phrasal Verbs Versus Compound Nouns derived from phrasals.

Phrasal verbs (that is, two-word or two-part verbs) are generally made up of a verb and preposition. For many of these, correct word stress is especially important as they have compound noun counterparts. In the following examples, the words on the left are phrasal verbs. The words on the right are nouns.

let down	letdown
Look out	lookout
Print out	printout
turn on	turnon
make over	makeover

In phrasal verbs, the preposition gets the word stress. If they have a noun counterpart, however, it gets the stress on the first part.

Homographs

Homographs are words that are written the same way but pronounced differently. In English, there are many words that have the same spelling, but whose part of speech changes with the word stress. If you listen carefully, you will hear that the vowel sounds change depending on whether they are stressed or unstressed.

VERB	NOUN
record	record
progress	progress
present	present
permit	permit

Sentence Stress

Sentence stress is the music of spoken English. Like word stress, sentence stress can help you to understand spoken English, especially when spoken fast. Sentence stress is what gives English its **rhythm.** We saw that word stress is accent on **one syllable** within a **word**. Sentence stress is accent on **certain words** within a **sentence**.

Most sentences have two types of word:

Content words are the key words of a sentence. These are important words that carry the meaning of the sentence.

Structure words are not very important words. They are small, simple words that make the sentence correct grammatically. They give the sentence its correct form or 'structure'.

If you remove the structure words from a sentence, you will probably still understand the sentence. If you remove the content words from a sentence, you will **not** understand the sentence. The sentence will have no sense or meaning, devoid of content words.

Let us look at this message:

Will you **FIND** me **HOME** because I'm **COMING** to **LONDON**.

This sentence is not complete. It is not a 'grammatically correct' sentence. But we still understand it. The four words written in bold letters communicate the meaning of the message very well. Somebody wants you to **find** a **home** for them because they are **coming** to **London.** We can add a few words:

Will you **FIND** me a **HOME** because I am **COMING** to **LONDON**.

The new words do not really add any more information. But they make the message more correct grammatically. In the sentence, the four **key words** (find, home, coming, London) are accentuated or stressed. They are content words that indicate the meaning of the whole sentence.

Thus, we notice that in a sentence, the content words are stressed, while the structure words are unstressed. The time between stressed words is always the same.

Lets look at some more examples of sentence stress:

Example 1: He can leave on Sunday.

In this sentence, the stressed words HE, LEAVE, SUNDAY make the sentence meaningful.

On the other hand, when we use the negative form "can't" we tend to stress the fact that it is the negative form by also stressing "can't".

He can't leave on Sunday.

In this sentence, the stressed words are HE, CAN'T, LEAVE, SUNDAY. The word "can't" is stressed because it lends purpose to the sentence.

In stress-timed languages, such as English, there is a roughly equal amount of time between each stress in a sentence. Sentence stress is an important factor in fluency and accurate pronunciation.

Rhythm

Rhythm is a feature as well as a product of the phonological structure of English. The phonology of any language is a system, so that a change in one part of the system will affect some or all of the other parts.

English is a very rhythmical language, so that a learner who can maintain the rhythm of the language is more likely to sound both natural and fluent. The two components of the system, which have the greatest influence on rhythm, are sentence stress and the various features of connected speech, i.e, what happens to words when we put them in an utterance. Let us look at these phonological parts in a little detail.

Sentence Stress

In any sentence, some words carry a stress. These are the *'strong'* or *'lexical'* words (usually nouns, verbs, adjectives and adverbs).

The remaining words are *'grammatical'* words and are unstressed or *'weak'* (conjunctions, pronouns, prepositions, auxiliaries, articles). While the former lend meaning to the sentence, the latter merely join the various words of a sentence together.

Connected Speech

Speed is also a factor in fluency. When we speak quickly, we speak in groups of words, which are continuous and may not have pauses between them. This causes changes to the 'shape' of words. Unstressed words always sound different when used in a sentence as opposed to being said in isolation.

The most common features of connected speech are the weak forms of grammatical and some lexical words (*and, to, of, have, was, were*) and contractions, some of which are acceptable in written English (*can't, won't, didn't etc.).*

We therefore notice that rhythm is a product of sentence stress and what happens to the words and sounds between the stresses.

English phonology is an entire system by its own self. Learners cannot achieve a natural rhythm in speech without understanding the stress-timed nature of the language and the interrelated components of stress, connected speech and intonation.

Paying attention to these little details and mastering them is the first step towards improving pronunciation skills that serves as a huge helping hand while trying to master the art of flawless and fluent English speech.

■

LESSON 4

Phonemes and Phonetics

We shall now attempt to understand what are phonemic and phonetic symbols and now why an understanding of these symbols is required to gain a command over perfect English pronunciation.

First, we look at phonemic symbols and their importance in the English language. Subsequently, we shall turn our attention towards phonetic symbols.

Phonemic Symbols

A phoneme is the theoretical representation of a sound in human speech. It is a sound of a language as represented or imagined without reference to its position in a word or phrase. A phoneme is thus, the imagination of a sound in the most non-aligned form. A phoneme can be imagined as a family of related phones, known as allophones, that the speakers of a language think of, and hear or see, as being emphatically similar and differing only in the phonetic environment in which they occur.

A phonemically ideal alphabet is one that has a single symbol for each phoneme. Phonemic symbols are used to represent the sounds of the English language. They are important teaching tools that can be a major aid in improving pronunciation.

What is the Need For Phonemic Symbols?

The English alphabet has 26 letters but the British English has 44 sounds. As we are all aware, English spelling is not a reliable guide to accurate pronunciation. Words are not always pronounced as they are written. This is because of the following reasons:

Some letters have more than one sound, such as **wind** (with a **short i** sound) **and wind** (with a **long i** sound), **read** (with a **short e** sound) **and read** (with a **long e** sound).

At times, some letters are not pronounced at all. For example: **g** in **gnat, gnaw**; **k** in **know, knee, knife**; **h** in **honest, honesty**; **p** in **psychology, pneumonia**; **s** in **isle, island,** etc.

Different letters may represent the same sound. For example: **byte and bite; scene and seen; hear and here; their and there; feat and feet; heir and air,** etc.

Sometimes syllables indicated by the spelling are not pronounced at all. Some examples are flood; look, poor, enough, through, etc.

Therefore, we notice that the letters of the alphabet are not an accurate indicator to pronunciation. In fact, following the letters in a given word can often be a cause for poor and incorrect pronunciation.

Phonemic symbols come handy in such cases. These symbols are completely reliable as following them; you will be able to get the correct pronunciation of words. Each symbol represents one sound consistently.

Phonemic symbols help students to use dictionaries effectively. The second bit of information in dictionaries for English language learners is the word in phonemic symbols. It comes right after the word itself. Knowing phonemic symbols enables students to get the maximum information from dictionaries.

With the use of these symbols, students can become independent learners. They will be able to find out the pronunciation of a word by themselves, without seeking any help. These phonemic symbols also serve as a visual aid. Students can see that two words differ, or are the same, in pronunciation. For example, 'son' and sun' must be pronounced the same because the phonemic symbols are the same for both these words.

Examples of Phonemes in English Language

Let us look at some examples of phonemes in English language:

The consonants, like /p/ and /b/ are two such letters as are written consistently with one letter for each sound. Such as **p**layer, s**p**in, **b**at, **b**oy etc.

Some times "s' is pronounced as "z", as in "vision."

However, phonemes might not be so apparent in written English, such as when they are typically represented with combined letters, called diagraphs, like <sh> (pronounced /?/) or <ch> (pronounced /?/).

A **restricted phoneme** is a phoneme that can only occur in a certain environment. There are restrictions as to where it can occur. Some such examples include:

/h/ occurs only before vowels and at the beginning of a syllable, never at the end, as in honest, hightened, etc.

Under most interpretations, /w/ and /j/ occur only before a vowel, never at the end of a syllable, such as wet, wild, watch, just, jet, jute etc.

Phonetic Symbols

Phonetic symbols are the speech sounds that are used in human speech. Phonetics is a study of such sounds that deals with the sounds themselves rather than the contexts in which they are used in languages. Phones is another term of phonetic symbols or sounds. Phonetics has three branches:

- **Articulatory phonetics:** concerned with position and movement of lips, tongue, vocal tract and speech organs.

- **Acoustic phonetics:** concerned with the properties of sound waves and how they are received by the inner ear.
- **Auditory phonetics:** concerned with speech perception, mainly how the brain forms perceptual representations of the input it receives.

Phonetic symbols are a great help when it comes to learning how to pronounce English words correctly. Any time you open a dictionary, you can find the correct pronunciation of words you do not know by looking at the phonetic pronunciation that follows the word. Unfortunately, learning the phonetic alphabet is not always the easiest thing to do.

In English language many words have the same pronunciation but are written differently and have different meanings. For example, 'to', 'two', and 'too', all have the phonetic transcription /tu/. Sometimes, words can be written similarly but have different pronunciations as in the 'ough' combinations, like thought, though, bough and through.

Another factor in pronunciation is how the word is stressed. Understanding the phonetic alphabet can greatly simplify the learning process, especially for students who do not have the opportunity to work.

The International Phonetic Association (IPA) has devised and developed an International Phonetic Alphabet, with an aim to provide a uniform and universally understood system for transcribing the speech sounds of all languages. English, just like other languages, too has an International Phonetic Alphabet that has been developed in order to aid accurate pronunciation skills in this very tricky and often confusing language.

If we notice the phonetic chart given below, we observe that the phonetic alphabet seems like another language entirely, however, with patience, it can serve us well in improving pronunciation and conversational skills.

The slashes and brackets around the phonetic symbols are not part of the IPA itself, language professionals have adopted them to distinguish between two main types of transcription, phonemic and phonetic. In phonemic transcriptions, the observer uses slashes to record the phonemes that the speakers target when they pronounce a word.

The brackets and slashes also clarify that their contents are not normal text, but a transcription. Because some IPA transcriptions can look like another word, the distinction is important.

Now, lets look at the phonetic symbols chart:

Vowels

i as in tree /tri/

ɪ as in insect /ɪnsekt/

ɛ as in bet /bɛt/

æ as in cat /kæt/

ɑ as in car /kɑ/ British /kɑr/ American

ɒ as in bought /bɒt/

ɔ as in saw /sɔ/

ʊ as in foot /fʊt/

u as in boot /but/

ʌ as in up /ʌp/

ɜ as in fur /fɜ/ British /fɜr/ American

ə as in ago /əˈgəʊ/

eɪ as in play /pleɪ/

əʊ as in know /nəʊ/

aɪ as in sky /skaɪ/

aʊ as in how /haʊ/

ɔɪ as in boy /bɔɪ/

ɪə as in near /nɪə/ British /nɪər/ American

eə as in where /weə/ British /weər/ American

ʊə as in pure /pjʊə/ British /pjʊər/ American

Consonants

p as in play /pleɪ/

b as in boy /bɔɪ/

t as in tree /tri/

d as in dog /dɒg/

k as in cat /kæt/

g as in got /gɒt/

tʃ as in chin /tʃɪn/

dʒ as in judge /dʒʊdʒ/

f as in fine /faɪn/

v as in visit /vɪzət/

θ as in thin /θɪn/

ð as in then /ðɛn/

s as in sick /sɪk/

z as in zoo /zu/

ʃ as in shine /ʃaɪn/

ʒ as in vision /viʒn/

h as in how /haʊ/

m as in much /mʌtʃ/

n as in now /naʊ/

ŋ as in sing /siŋ/

l as in leg /lɛg/

r as in read /rid/ or /rɛd/

j as in yes /jɛs/

w as in wet /wɛt/

The phonemic and phonetic symbols guide us towards an accurate pronunciation of different words. A working knowledge of these symbols is important in order to perfect pronunciation skills in English.

Thus, in this section on pronunciation skills, we learnt that pronunciation in English language comprises of three components. First is the physical ability to articulate the correct sounds, which implies, knowledge about where to place your tongue and how to read out each word. Second is the use of stress, that is, which syllables to stress in a word and what words to stress in a sentence. Third and last is use of pitch, rhythm and fluency.

Knowledge of phonetic and phonemic symbols helps us with the ability to read and pronounce the accurate sounds of words. This is important because English is a tricky language and all words are not pronounced as they are written. Information about word and sentence stress helps us to learn what syllables to stress in a word and which ones to skip over. Stressing the right words is important because it makes our spoken English easy to comprehend and pleasant to listen. The use of rhythm, pitch and fluency helps us to make our speech rhythmical and agreeable to our listeners.

Now, that we have learnt how to polish skills in English pronunciation, let us turn towards mastering Englsih vocabulary and grammar.

■

PART II

BASIC ENGLISH GRAMMAR

Importance of Learning Grammar Rules

Many people wonder what is the need for grammar lessons? Knowledge of grammar is imperative to acquiring above par conversational skills. Grammar lessons are very important in providing information to the learner about grammar rules and its usage.

Good grammatical understanding and knowledge is important in order to communicate clearly and to get the real meaning across to the listener. Grammatical errors can lead to misunderstandings and may lead the listener to misunderstand the speaker. Proper grammar, on the other hand, prevents misunderstandings and misconceptions, while ensuring that your thoughts and ideas get across appropriately.

Proper and complete grammatical knowledge is indispensable for good written and oral skills. Writing and speaking clearly, without any grammatical errors makes the user come across as credible and reliable. If we look around, we would notice that experts in various professions and occupations, like business leaders and political heads, are able to communicate clearly and accurately in both written as well as spoken English. Thus, for those striving to build their reputation in their respective spheres, flawless written and oral skills in English are very important.

Good grammatical knowledge and understanding is very often

believed to be synonymous with good education and above average intelligence. Strangers and people we meet for the first time, often judge us on the basis of our fluency and accuracy in speech. Poor communication skills and an under-developed grammatical knowledge can often lead strangers to judge us poorly.

Thus, we see how important it is to be conversant with grammar rules. Though, a lot of people are keen to improve their grammatical knowledge, they are often unable to do so because unfortunately, there are no shortcuts available. In order to be well versed with proper grammar skills, it is important to devote the necessary time and approach the subject with total dedication and commitment.

In the following pages, we shall attempt to understand grammar rules and endeavour to gain some measure of proficiency in them.

■

Lesson 5

Nouns and Pronouns

Nouns

Definition: Noun may be defined as the name of a person, place, animal or thing. For example: **Bill Jones**, **Geneva**, **donkey** and **computer** are all examples of nouns that we commonly come across in our daily lives.

Examples:

London is the capital city of **United Kingdom**.

George Bush is the President of **USA**.

Democracy is a government for the **people**, of the **people** and by the **people**.

Kinds of Nouns: There are five different kinds of nouns.

- *Proper Noun* is used to denote a particular person, place or thing. Some examples of proper nouns are:

Bill Jones is a dear friend of mine.

We recently visited **Geneva** during summer vacation.

English is a popular language in the **Carribean**.

The words written in bold letters are all proper nouns. As we notice, the first letter of these words is always written in capital letters.

- *Common Noun* is used to refer to other things and beings

that signify a class by themselves. Let us look at some examples:

I saw a **monkey** jump over the **bridge**.

A **computer** is a wonderful device.

Unlike the proper nouns, the common nouns do not begin with capital letters.

- *Collective Noun* is used to refer to a collection of things. For example:

The **jury** reviewed the report before giving its final verdict.

Look at that **flock** of birds flying high in the sky.

- *Material Noun* is used to denote the substance with which things are made. Examples are:

This table is made of ***wood.***

The bracelet that I am wearing is cast in pure ***gold.***

- *Abstract Noun* is used for a state or a quality possessed by a person or thing. Some examples are:

I was impressed by his **honesty**.

Laughter is the best medicine.

Nouns may also be classified as countable and uncountable nouns.

- *Countable Nouns* are those nouns that denote anything that can be counted. For example:

Europe and Asia are **two** widely different continents.

On his way back home, he was surrounded by **four** highway thieves.

- *Uncountable Nouns*, also known as mass nouns, are used to refer to things that cannot be counted. Let us clarify with some examples:

Robin expressed **grief** at the untimely demise of Drake's father.

United Nations aims to maintain international **peace**.

On the basis of number, nouns may also be categorised as singular and plural. ***Singular*** is used to denote a single object, such as knife, monkey, speciality, etc. ***Plural,*** on the other hand, refers to two or more objects, such as knives, monkeys, specialities, etc.

- *Forms of Nouns*: Nouns can also be **subjective, objective and possessive**.Let us cleaify this with some examples:

The **English teacher** was an elegant lady, with an excellent command over the language. (subjective case)

The **English teacher's** car was always parked in the school playground. (possessive case)

Students choose the **English teacher** as the teacher of the year. (objective case)

- ***Noun Clause***: contains a subject and verb and can do anything that a noun can do.

Example: What she does for this institute is really praiseworthy.

- ***Noun Phrase*:** has two parts- one part contains a noun and the other part could be an adjective, a participial phrase, an infinitive phrase, a modifying phrase or a preposition.

Examples: (a) Several incidents have been reported of train burglaries.

A story is often told that he was once a lieutenant in the Indian armed forces.

The first part of these sentences is a noun and the second part is a modifier.

Pronouns

***Definition*:** Pronouns are often used to replace nouns and to make sentences and speech less repetitive and less cumbersome.

Examples:

We are going out to a discotheque.

Her dress is the trendiest dress I have ever seen.

This is my house.

What are **you** doing here?

The words written in bold letters are pronouns.

Kinds of Pronouns: There are seven different kinds of pronouns.

- ***Personal Pronoun*** is used to refer to specific persons or things and its form changes to accommodate gender, number, person and case.

Subjective Personal Pronoun is used in cases where the pronoun acts as the subject of the sentence. Such as:

He stole my bag and ran away with it.

They are coming tomorrow for dinner.

Possessive Personal Pronoun indicates that the pronoun is being used to mark a particular possession and is used to define who owns a specific object or thing. For example:

This is the dearest possession of **mine**.

His book is in the cupboard.

Objective Personal Pronoun is used to indicate that the pronoun is acting as an object of a verb or preposition, etc. Some examples are:

Joan will meet **us** in the market.

James was thrilled to see **her** at the competition.

- ***Demonstrative Pronoun*** is used to point to a noun or a pronoun and to identify the noun or pronoun. Excamples are:

This is my hat.

That is the watch he bought for me.

These are his books.

Those are her accessories.

"This" and "that" are used for singular nouns, whereas, "These" and "those" are used for plural nouns.

- ***Interrogative Pronoun*** is used to form questions. Whom, whose, which, what are examples of interrogative pronouns.

Examples:

Who finished the race first?

Whose watch is this?

Who, whom, whose and, at times, which are used to refer to people. Which and what are used to refer to animals and objects.

- ***Relative Pronoun*** may be used to link a clause or phrase to another clause or phrase, such as, whom, whomever, which and whichever. Let us look at some examples:

You may pick **whichever** dress you wish to.

The man **who** stole Rebecca's necklace has been put behind the bars.

The primary difference between interrogative and relative pronouns is that while the former are used to form questions, the latter are used to connect different clauses and phrases in a given sentence.

- ***Indefinite Pronoun*** is used to refer to an identifiable person or object, but the person or object is not specified. Examples include: all, few, any, anyone, every, everyone, anything, everything, many, none, nobody, etc.

Many were invited to the party but only a **few** came.

The teacher passed a copy of the latest syllabus to **everyone** in the class.

- ***Reflexive Pronoun*** is often used to refer back to the subject of the sentence or the clause.

Examples:

The teacher read out the chapter **herself** so that the students could concentrate on understanding the concept.

You should try and educate **yourself**.

- ***Intensive Pronoun*** is used to refer to its antecedent (what precedes the intensive pronoun). It is identical to reflexive pronoun. Some examples are:

I **myself** finished the entire house work.

He **himself** promised to be present at the dinner, even though he has an early morning flight to catch.

Some Important Points:

- *Us* and *We* always used in relation to a noun.
- *Than* and *As* are used to compare objects, places or persons.
- A pronoun always has only one antecedent and should not refer to an implied idea.
- A pronoun should not refer to a title.
- It must not be used to refer to possessive nouns or adjectives.
- Remember that *They*, *Those* refer to plural objects or persons. *It*, *That* refer to singular objects.
- *Who* is used to refer to a person and *Which* is used for things and animals.

■

LESSON 6

Adjectives and Verbs

Adjectives

Definition: Adjectives are used to describe nouns or pronouns. The articles *a, an, the* are also adjectives.

Examples:

This is a **powerful** motor.

This motor is **more powerful** than many of the motors available today.

This motor is the **most powerful** of all motors.

Degrees of Adjectives: Adjectives may appear in three degrees.

Positive Degree: Examples are: strong, long, powerful, etc.

Comparitive Degree: these adjectives generally end in suffix –er or are prefixed by "more". Examples: stronger, longer, more powerful etc.

Superlative Degree: such adjectives are prefixed by "most" or end in suffix –est. Examples include: strongest, longest, most powerful, etc.

Let us look at some more examples:

Positive	**Comparitive**	**Superlative**
Poor	Poorer	Poorest

Good	Better	Best
Bad	Worse	Worst
Far	Further	Furthest
Little	Less	Least

Good, bad, far and *little* are some examples of adjectives that occur in irregular comparitive and superlative forms. There are some adjectives that do not conform to the comparitive form, such as *ideal, absolute, final, universal, whole, preferrable,* etc.

Some Important Points:

- Adjectives should not be confused with possessives, which signify possession. Example: *girls party* and *girls' party*: former is an adjective and the latter is a possessive.
- Adjectives should not be mixed with participles, which symbolise verb forms ending in –ed and -ing.

  Example: He is a *scared* child and He is a *scaring* child.

  The students were *confused* and The puzzle was *confusing*.

  In these examples, *scared* and *confused* are participles, while *scaring* and *confusing* are adjectives. While the former are verb forms and signify the act performed by *the child (*i.e. he is scared) and by *the students* (the students were confused), the latter describe the state of the *child* (he is a scaring child) and the quality of the *puzzle* (the puzzle was confusing).

  If confronted with such situations of adjectives along with possessives and participles, you should try asking yourself what function does a particular word perform: is it to indicate possession, is it a verb form or is it to describe a state or quality of a person or an object?
- There are also A-adjectives, which appear as predicates in sentences, following a linking verb.

  Examples: He was *alone* at home.

The house was *ablaze*.

With a great difficult, Roger managed to keep *afloat*.

Adjective Clauses contain a subject and a verb and can do anything that an adjective can do.

Examples: My friends *who attended the party* had a great time.

The prawns *that Julia cooked* looked delicious.

The man *whose baby cried* in the movie hall was sitting next to me.

Verbs

Definition: Verbs are words used to describe actions.

Examples:

I **am reading** a book.

I want **to read** this book fully.

She is **working** in a bank.

If she earned better, she would have bought her own house.

Types of Verbs: Verbs can be divided into three categories:

- *Normal verbs*: These are the most common type of verbs and are used to denote actions that we see people around us performing all the time. These can be used in any tense form.

Examples:

I *eat* breakfast every day.

I am *eating* breakfast now.

Jane wants *to go* to the party.

Jane is *going* to the party.

- *Non-continuous verbs* are used to denote things that we can not see others doing.

Examples: He wants *to live* life to the fullest.

She *owns* this house.

I like *to share* my joys with others.

- ***Mixed verbs***: have more than one meaning. Some meanings function as normal verbs and some as non-continuous verbs.

Examples: Rajan *appears* confused. (Non-continuous verb)

My favourite rock star is *appearing* in a stage show tonight. (Normal verb)

Apart from these three categories, verbs may be conditional, active, passive and also phrasal.

- ***Conditional Verbs***: are used to talk about possibilities and unreal situations that do not exist right now but may appear in future or existed in the past.

Examples: *If I had more money*, I would have bought this house.

If Roger had studied harder, he would have passed the exam.

- ***Active Verbs:*** In active sentences, the thing doing the action is the subject of the sentence and the thing receiving the action is the object.

Examples: John is cooking food.

The teacher is teaching the students.

In the first sentence, *John* is the subject, the *food* is the object and *cooking* is the active verb. In the second sentence, *the teacher* is the subject, *the students* are the object and *teaching* is the active verb.

- ***Passive Verbs:*** In passive sentences, the thing receiving the action is the subject of the sentence and the thing doing the action is optionally included near the end of the sentence. The passive form may also be used if you think that the thing receiving the action is more important or should be emphasised. You can also use the passive form if you do not know who is doing the action or if you do not want to mention who is doing the action.

Examples:

The food is cooked by John.

The students are taught by the teacher.

In the first sentence, *the food* is the subject receiving the action, *John* is doing the action and the verb is *cooked*. Similarly, in the second sentence, *the students* are the subjects receiving the action, *the teacher* is doing the action and the passive verb is *taught*.

- ***Phrasal Verbs*** are idiomatic expressions, combining verbs and prepositions to form new words. For example, the verb *ask* when combined with a preposition *out, in* or *after* can denote meanings different from the dictionary meaning of *ask*.

Ask out means invite or connect or join, such as, John *asked out* Jane for a date.

Ask in means inviting some one into your house, such as, Mrs. Clinton *asked* me *in* her house.

Ask after means to enquire about some one's health, such as, I *asked after* the teacher's health from her daughter.

- ***Transitive Verbs and Intransitive Verbs***: Transitive verbs are those verbs that can be used to form complete and meaningful sentences, even without the use of an object.

Examples:

Sharon laughs.

The teacher teaches.

- ***Intransitive verbs*** are those verbs that are used along with an object in order to form comprehensible sentences.

Examples: Sharon writes a letter.

The teacher teaches a lesson.

■

LESSON 7

Adverbs and Prepositions

Adverbs

Definition: Adverbs are words used to modify verbs, adjectives or other verbs. These words often tell when, where, why, or under what conditions something happens or happened and frequently end in *–ly*.

Examples: You must finish this work **quickly.**

I have never **visited the desert** but he lives **there**.

I cook food **occasionally** but she cooks it **daily.**

Kinds of Adverbs: There are five kinds of adverbs.

Adverbs of Manner: George speaks **softly** and **politely.**

In this sentence, the adverbs *softly* and *politely* signify the manner in which George speaks.

Adverbs of Place: I have lived **on the island** all my life.

I still live **there.**

In these sentences, the adverbs are used to denote the place, *on the island* and *there*.

Adverbs of Frequency: She feeds the birds **every day**.

She **seldom** goes with some one.

In these sentences the adverbs are used to denote the frequency.

Adverbs of Time: signify time.

Examples: He tries to finish his dinner **before dark.**

He is finishing his dinner **now.**

He is finishing his dinner ***early*** today.

Adverb of Purpose: It denotes the purpose.

Examples: She eats food slowly **to digest it properly**.

She reads spiritual books **to draw some learning**.

***Viewpoint Adverb*:** It generally follows a noun and is related to the adjective that precedes the noun.

Examples: It investing all our money in mutual funds is not a sound idea *financially*.

***Focus Adverb*:** It indicates what is being communicated is limited to the part that is focused; a focus adverb will tend either to limit the sense of the sentence or to act as an addictive.

Example: She gets an A grade in all her tests.

Negative Adverb: It is used to create a negative meaning, without the use of no/never/neither constructions.

Examples: She *seldom* calls.

He *hardly* comes to our house.

Relative Adverbs: *Where, when* and *why* are relative adverbs. These are used some times to introduce adjectival clauses. The clause in such cases is adjectival and modifies a noun, the relative words performs an adverbial function.

Examples:

She stays in this big house **where** her grandfather lived.

In this sentence, *where* begins a clause that modifies the noun *house*.

This is the time of the year **when** several migratory birds come to our country.

In this sentence, *when* is used to modify time.

Do you know **why** she seems so worked up all the time?

Why, in this sentence, is used to modify reason.

Adverb Phrases: They are combination words consisting of an adverb and a preposition or an infinitive.

Examples:

The man who lives *next door* is a renowned preacher.

I am saving money *to renovate my house*.

The first sentence contains a preposition *next* and the second sentence contains an infinitive *to*.

Adverb Clauses: They contain a subject, a verb and an adverb.

Examples: *Wherever there is a population problem*, there is poverty and unemployment.

After it rains, the weather will become pleasant.

Prepositions

Definition: A preposition is used to describe relationship between words in a sentence.

Examples:

I live **in** this house.

She sleeps **at** noon and **at** night.

I read books **for** gaining knowledge.

Different Types of Prepositions:

Prepositions of Time: They are used to denote time such as *at*, *on* or *in*.

Examples:

The train arrived **on** time.

The flight is scheduled **at** 07:30 a.m. tomorrow.

She studies **in** this class.

Prepositions of Place: They are used for specific places, such as *at*, *on* or *in*.

Examples:

She is staying **at** Hotel Inter-Continental **in** Sydney.

Her house is **on** Temple Street.

Prepositions of Position: They indicate the position of a particular object or thing, such as *at*, *on* or *in*.

Examples:

I will see you **at** work tomorrow.

She jumped **on** the bed.

She found the book she wanted ***in*** the library.

Prepositions of Movement: They are used to denote movement of objects or persons, such as *to* or *towards*.

Examples:

I am going **to** the bank.

She was heading **towards** total disaster.

Let us move **toward** light.

Prepositions of Time: They are used to denote to measure time, such as *for* or to refer to a particular date or time, such as *since*.

Examples:

I have been working **for** five years in this company.

I have been working in this company **since** June 2000.

Some Important Points:

- Often prepositions occur along with nouns, such as *belief in*, *concern for*, *disapproval of.*
- Some times, they occur along with adjectives, like *familiar with, worried about, afraid of.*
- Prepositions may also occur along with verbs, such as *give up, apologise for, worry about.*
- Some words even though they may appear to be prepositions are not actually prepositions, such as *downstairs, downtown, upstairs, uptown, inside* and *outside,* etc.
- Often prepositions are used to form idiomatic expressions, like *agree to* a proposal, *argue about* a matter, *correspond to*, *differ from,* etc.

■

Lesson 8

Conjunctions and Interjections

Conjunctions

Definition: A conjunction is a word that joins parts of a sentence.

Examples:

Roger **and** David are good friends, **but** they do not get along with James.

Wherever you go,I will accompany you.

As we are going out of town, we will not be able to join you for dinner tonight.

Types of Conjunctions:

Co-ordinating Conjunctions: such as *and, but, or, yet, so, nor, for*.

Examples:

I reached there on time, *but* he had not arrived.

This book is *for* you.

George *and* Charles are good friends.

Some times, co-ordinating conjunctions connect two independent clauses, they are often accompanied by a comma, for example in the first sentence, given above.

Subordinating Conjunctions: They occur at the beginning of a subordinate clause and establish its relationship with the rest of the sentence, such as *even though, because, unless, wherever, after,* etc.

Examples:

He came *after* she arrived.

It is important to alter unhealthy lifestyle *because* it can lead to serious diseases.

I will not come *unless* he comes to pick me up.

Some Important Points:

- Distincion between *like* and *as*: *Like* is a preposition and may be used to introduce a prepositional phrase, but should not be used to introduce a clause. *As*, on the other extreme, is a conjunction.
- *That* is used as a conjunction to link a subordinate clause to a preceding verb. However, often we notice that this word is omitted in order to strike a good effect.

Example:

Rebecca knew that she is about to receive the award.

Remember that we did not have enough manpower and resources when we started this company.

These sentences would definitely sound better and pleasant if the *that* is omitted, like:

Remember we did not have enough manpower and resources when we started this company.

- Some conjunctions occur with other words to form corelative conjunctions.

Examples:

He led his team *not only* by experience *but also* by example.

Neither Isabella *nor* Rebecca appeared for the final exams.

- Some conjunctions are used together with adverbs and are referred to as conjunctive adverbs. Examples include *moreover, however, consequently*, *nevertheless, as a result,* etc.

Interjections

Definition: An interjection is a word added to a sentence to convey emotion. It is not grammatically related to any part of the sentence and is usually succeeded by an exclamation mark.

Examples:

Hey! Come here.

Oouch! That hurts.

■

LESSON 9

Verbals in English Language

English language has three kinds of verbals: participles, infinitives and gerunds. These are also known as non-finites that have no subject, no tense and do not accept any modal verbs.

Participles work as adjectives, gerunds as nouns and infinitives have noun-like, verb-like and adjective-like functions.

Let us look at each of these in detail.

Participles

Definition: Participles are verbal adjectives that describe a noun. They usually precede the noun that they modify. They may also be linked to the subject of the sentence by a linking verb such as *to be* or *to feel.*

Participles in a sentence may be components in multipart verb or may function as adjectives or nouns.

Examples:

Mrs. Jones **was beating** our pet dog with a broom to retrieve her pet chick.

This sentence serves as an example of a participle, *was beating* used as a component in multiverb.

Midnight is a **frightening** time to venture alone.

Here, the participle *frightening* is used as an adjective to describe and modify the noun *midnight*.

James hates **cooking** eggs because their foul smell puts him off.

In this sentence, the participle, *cooking* also serves as a noun.

She felt **frightened** as she walked alone at midnight.

In the above sentence, *frightened* serves as an adjective.

Kinds of Participles: There are generally two kinds of participles: present participle and past participle.

Present Participle: It is formed by adding the suffix –ing to the verb, such as interesting, frightening, fulfilling, etc.

Exceptions: the final *–e* is dropped: coming, whistling

The last consonant after a stressed vowel is doubled: sitting, dropping

Final consonant after a vowel is doubled: travelled, rubbing.

Final *ie* changes to *y*: lying, worrying.

Present participles also serve as adjectives, modifying the nouns that affect some one or some thing.

Examples:

This is an **interesting** lesson.

Midnight is a **frightening** time to be alone.

It is also used along with the verbs *to be* and *to have* to create verb tenses.

Past Participle: It is generally formed by adding the suffix –ed to the verb, such as interested, frightened, fulfilled, etc.

However, there are some irregular forms of past participles as well. Let us look at these:

Ending in *–d*: danced, confused, excited, etc.

Final consonant after a vowel is doubled: travelled, rubbed

Final consonant after a short stressed vowel is doubled: admitted

Last *y* after a consonant becomes *i*: hurried, worried

As adjectives, past participles may be used to modify nouns that are affected by someone or something.

Examples:

The students were **interested** in the new lesson.

She was **frightened** to walk alone at midnight.

It may also be used with verbs *to be* and *to have* to create verb tenses, just like the present participle.

Infinitive

Definition: Infinitive is the name for some verb forms that exist in certain languages, such as English. Infinitive of a verb refers to the basic form of the verb without the participle. Some examples are *be, to be, do, to do* and *therefore*.

Examples: He likes **to do** this work.

She is going **to be** present there.

Will she **be** there?

In these sentences, we notice that infinitives are often introduced by *to*. Such infinitives are known as full infinitives or simple infinitives. However, there are also cases when *to* is absent. In such cases, the infinitive is considered to be a bare infinitive.

Words like *see, watch, sense, feel, hear* are examples of bare infinitives.

Examples: I **see** a plane in the sky.

I **heard** this happening.

He can **sense** that something is wrong.

Gerund

Definition: A gerund functions as a verbal noun in English language. In English, it is similar to the present participle, ending in *–ing*. It often functions as a verb within a clause and the clause as a whole functions as a noun in the sentence.

Example: **Playing** cricket is my favourite pastime.

Learning English is very easy.

Some times, gerunds and infinitives may be used in sentences without any change in meaning.

Examples: I like **to work.**

I like **working.**

She prefers **to sleep** rather than **to watch** television.

She prefers **sleeping** rather than **watching** television.

However, in some other cases, their use can drastically change the meaning of a sentence.

Examples: I dread meeting her.

I dread to think what she will say.

Some Important Points:

- Infinitives and gerunds may be used as subjects of a sentence.

Examples:

To read out scriptures to his grandmother is his daily chore.

Reading out aloud helps to understand word pronunciation.

As we observe in the above-mentioned sentence, a *to*-infinitive may also appear as the subject of a sentence. However, it is more common for this infinitive to appear as a subject complement.

Examples:

Her favourite pastime is **to read** philisophical books.

He likes **to watch** planes in the sky.

- A gerund may also, like the *to*-infinitive, be used as a subject complement.

Examples:

Her favourite pastime is **reading** philiosophical books.

He likes **watching** planes in the sky.

- Infinitives and gerunds can help identify certain nouns and in such cases they function as noun complement.

Examples:

Her desire **to watch the cricket match** live became a demand.

Her ardent desire, **watching the cricket match live**, became a stubborn demand.

- In some cases, infinitives follow certain adjectives and in such instances, the infinitive is said to be functioning as an adjective complement.

Examples:

She was adamant **to watch** the cricket match.

He was reluctant **to go** back home.

- Gerunds can often be seen in the role of objects of preposition. However, there are hardly any infinitives that fit in this category.

Examples:

The student thanked his teacher **for** helping him cope with the pressure.

- Prepositions, *except* and *but* can occasionally be used with infinitives.

Examples:

The workers had no choice **but** to agree to the terms of the management.

What alternative do we have **except** to leave gracefully?

■

PART III

FUNCTIONAL GRAMMAR

Having looked at and understood basic grammar concepts, let us now turn to lessons in functional grammar. Functional grammar comprises of basic grammar concepts and yet these basic grammar concepts would really mean nothing devoid of tenses, articles and punctuation, etc.

In this section, we shall focus on grammar at work. The basic grammar lessons that we learnt in the previous section, require added functional features in order to be used. Without these functional features, like articles and tenses, etc., no sentences or speech can be formed and any grammar learning would be incomplete without a study of these features.

In this section on Functional Grammar, we shall study tense forms, articles, determiners, quantifiers, modals, voice, narration, punctuation, phrases, clauses and sentences.

■

LESSON 10

Tenses

Definition: Tense is a form of verb which shows the time of an action and its degree of completeness.

Examples: I **am writing** a novel.

I **was writing** a novel.

I **will be writing** a novel.

Types of Tenses: There are three main kinds of tenses: **present**, **past** and **future** tense, which have further sub-types. Let us look at these types and their sub-types in detail.

Present Tense is used to denote an action that is taking place now.

Examples: The train **is leaving**.

Joan **knows** French.

Sub-Types:

Simple Present These tenses follow the form verb + s/es.

Examples: She **drinks** water.

The train to Switzerland **leaves** tomorrow at 6:00 a.m.

Different Uses:

- It is used to convey the idea that an action is repetitive or usual. It can be a habit, a daily chore or a scheduled event.

Examples: I **eat** food.

She **eats** food.

He **does not eat** food.

- Simple present tense is also used to make generalisations or indicate a fact.

  Examples: London **is** the capital of United Kingdom.

  Parrots **like** green chillies.

- It can also be used to talk about scheduled events in the near future.

  Examples: What time **does** the lecture begin tomorrow?

  The bus **leaves** tomorrow at 8:15 p.m.

- Simple present tense may also be used to indicate that an action is happening or not happening now.

  Examples: I **am reading** a book now.

  She **is not reading** a book.

Present Continuous follows the form am/is/are+present participle.

Examples:

She **is studying** now.

He **is meeting** you after work today.

Diffferent Uses:

- It can be used with normal verbs to convey the idea that some thing is happening now, or not happening now at this moment.

  Examples: He **is sleeping** now.

  She **is watching** a play.

  I **am not sleeping** now.

- It may be used for a longer action that is in process and may take a day, a month, a year or even a century to complete.

Examples: Rochel **is saving** money to repay his mortgage loan.

He **is not working** these days.

- It may even be used to indicate something that may or may not happen in the near future.

  Examples: Cecilia **is not coming** to the party tonight.

  I **am meeting** my college friends today after lunch.

- Present continuous tense used along with words like *always* or *constantly* denotes that some thing irrating or unpleasant is happening.

  Examples: He **is always irritating** with his silly questions.

  She **is constantly talking** non-stop.

Present Perfect follows the pattern has/have+past participle.

Examples:

I **have travelled** to Europe many times.

My son **has learnt** French.

Different Uses:

- Present perfect tense is used to describe an action that occurred at an unspecified time before now. The exact time in such cases is not important. Some examples are *ever, never, once, many times, several times, before, already,* etc.

  Examples: I **have met** him several times.

  She **has never** travelled outside this country.

  Susan **has not arrived** as yet.

- It may be used to describe an experience you may have had, but not to talk about specific events.

  Examples: Joan **has been** to London.

  Joan **has been** to London four times.

  I think that I **have seen** this place before.

- It may be used to talk about an experience that has happened over a period of time.

  Examples: My French has really **improved** since I moved to Paris.

- It can be used to talk about achievements of an individual and humanity.

  Examples: My daughter **has learnt** how to speak.

  Scientists **have found** cure for many diseases.

- It is also used to talk about an action that was anticipated, but has not happened.

  Examples: Susan **has not finished** her holiday home work as yet.

  It **has not rained** in this desert for many years.

- It is also used to talk about multiple actions that have occured in the past.

  Examples: Invaders **have plundered** this area several times in search of diamonds and other precious stones.

  Karen **has consulted** four doctors, but not one has been able to identify the cause for her sickness.

- Present perfect may be used to talk about an event that happened in our lives before now. It may even be used to limit the time in experience.

  Examples: **Have** you **read** any book in the last month?

  She **has read** this book three times.

  I **have visited** five places in the last one year.

- It is used in combination with non-continuous verbs or non-continuous uses of mixed verbs to denote some thing that started in the past and has continued uptil now.

  Examples: She **has had** flu for one week .

  He **has shifted** to London for the past seven months.

- Present perfect tense is also used for active and passive verbs.

  Examples: Many of my friends **have seen** this movie. (Active)

  This movie **has been seen** by many of my friends. (Passive)

<u>**Present Perfect Continuous Tense**</u> follows the pattern has/have+been+present participle.

Examples:

I **have been living** in this house for ten years now.

He **has been working** on this project for over one month.

Different Uses:

- Present perfect continuous tense is used to talk about some thing that happened in the past and has continued uptil now.

  Examples: The plumbers **have been digging** water for the last five days.

  He **has been working** in this organisation for the last ten years.

- It can also be used without a duration, such as *lately, recently*.

  Examples: I **have been feeling** very sick lately.

  Recently, **he has been working** with an event management firm.

<u>**Past Tense**</u> is used to denote an action that has already taken place in the past.

Examples: He **cooked** food for us yesterday.

He **cooked** the dinner, *washed* the utensils and *cleaned* up the kitchen.

Sub-Types:

<u>**Simple Past**</u> follows the pattern verb+ed or irregular verbs.

Examples:

We **watched** a movie yesterday.

He has **read** this book already.

Different Uses:

- Simple past tense is used to refer to a completed action in the past, an action which started and was finished in the past.

  Examples: We **went** out for dinner yesterday.

  We **didn't go** out for dinner yesterday.

- It is also used to list a series of actions, such as action 1,2,3 and so on that were completed in the past.

  Examples: I **found** the book I was looking for, **read** it and **returned** it to the librarian.

  She **reached** Paris in the morning, **attended** the seminar at noon, **finished** shopping by evening and **went** back the next day morning.

- Another use is to indicate an action that started and stopped in the past.

  Examples: I **worked** in this company for two years.

  He **lived** here for ten years befor he **went** to America.

- It is also used to describe a habit that started and stopped in the past.

  Examples: He **learnt** salsa when he was a teenager.

  He **never learnt** salsa when he was a teenager.

- It may also be used to describe past facts or generalisations that are no longer true.

  Examples: He **was** an introvert child, but now he is an extrovert.

I **lived** in Los Angeles before.

- Use in Active/Passive:

  Examples: Tina cooked the dinner. (Active)

  The dinner was cooked by Tina. (Passive)

Past Continuous occurs in the form was/were + present participle.

Examples:

Mother **was cooking** when I reached home.

They **were leaving** tonight but something very unfortunate happened.

Different Uses:

- Past continuous tense is used to indicate that a longer action in the past was interrupted.

  Examples: He **was studying** when the guests came.

  While we **were enjoying** an outdoor party, it began raining.

- It may also be used to denote a specific time as interruption.

  Examples: He **was studying** at 7:00 p.m., when the guests called.

  While we **were enjoying** an outdoor party at 8:30 p.m., it began raining.

  It should be noted that while simple past shows when an action began or stopped, past continuous is used to denote a specific time when the action was interrupted.

- It is also used with two actions in the same sentence to convey the idea that both actions were occuring simultaneously.

  Examples: He **was studying**, while his mother **was cooking** dinner.

  We **were eating** lunch, **remembering** good old days and **having** a great time.

- It is also used to describe a series of parallel action in the past, to create an atmosphere.

  Examples: When I visited the Jones, Mrs. Jones **was cooking** food, Julia **was playing** the piano and Johny **was reading** a book.

- Past continuous tense is used with *always* and *constantly* to convey the idea that something annoying, shocking or irritating happened in the past.

  Examples: He **was constantly talking** nonstop.

  James **was always coming** late to the class.

- When we talk about things in the past, *when* is followed by simple past tense and *while* is used with past continuous. *While* is used to convey the idea of during that time.

  Examples: Johny was sleeping, **when his friend called**.

  While Johny was sleeping, his friend called.

- Past continuous tense cannot be used for any non-continuous verbs.

  Examples: Roger **was being** at his house, when you called. (Incorrect)

  Roger **was** at his house, when you called. (Correct)

- Use in Active/Passive forms:

  Examples: I **was cooking** food when the doorbell rang. (Active)

  Food **was being cooked** by me when the doorell rang. (Passive)

<u>**Past Perfect**</u> follows the form had + past participle.

Examples:

She **had finished** studying when her father came home from work.

Mr. Jones **had completed** his work when his boss gave him another assignment.

Different Uses:

- The Past Perfect expresses the idea that something occurred before another action in the past. It can also show that something happened before a specific time in the past.

  Examples: I **had never seen** such a beautiful island before I went to Tioman.

  He did not have money because he **had lost** his wallet.

- With non-continuous verbs and with non-continuous uses of mixed verbs, the Past Perfect tense is used to show that something started in the past and continued up until another action in the past.

  Examples: We **had lived** in this house, before we purchased a new one.

  She felt bad about leaving her school because she **had studied** there for twelve years.

- It can be used with specific time words or phrases, unlike present perfect tense.

  Examples: I **had visited** Malaysia in 2002, before I permanently moved there in 2004.

- Past perfect may be used optionally with words *before* and *after*.

  Examples: I **had visited** Malaysia in 2002, before I permanently moved there in 2004.

  I **visited** Malaysia in 2002, before I permanently moved there in 2004.

  Both these sentences are correct.

- Use in Active/Passive Forms:

Examples: I **had visited** many countries before I visited Italy. (Active)

Many countries **had been visited** by me before I visited Italy. (Passive)

Past Perfect Continuous follows the pattern had been + present participle. The main distinction between past perfect continuous and past continuous is that while the latter refers to interrupted actions, the former emphasises a duration of time before something in the past.

Examples:

I **had been working** in this company for two years before I found another job.

He **had been living** in this house for ten years before his father bought him a new house.

Different Uses:

- We use the Past Perfect Continuous to show that something started in the past and continued up until another time in the past.

  Examples: We **had been chatting** over two hours before Tom arrived.

  Angelina **had been working** in this company for five years before she left this job for another.

- Using the Past Perfect Continuous before another action in the past helps to show cause and effect.

  Examples: Katie learnt dancing because she **had been practising** for a year.

  She lost weight because she **had been doing** aerobics regularly.

- Non-continuous verbs and non-continuous uses of mixed verbs cannot be used with past perfect continuous. Instead, in such cases, past perfect may be used.

Examples: This house **was belonging** to the Clintons before Mr. Jones bought it. (Incorrect)

This house **had belonged** to the Clintons before Mr. Jones bought it. (Correct)

<u>**Future Tense**</u> is used to refer to actions that will take place in the future.

Sub-Types:

<u>**Simple Future**</u> follows the pattern will + verb or am/is/are+going to +verb.

Examples: I **will meet** him later.

He **will study** tomorrow.

I **am going to meet** him later.

He **is not going to study** tomorrow.

Different Uses:

- Simple future tense (*will*) is used to express a voulntary action.

  Examples: I **will meet** him later.

  He **will study** tomorrow.

  Will is also used to express a promise.

  Examples: I **will call** him today.

  If I win the elections, I **will eradicate** poverty and unemployment.

  Be going is used to express an intended action.

  Examples: He **is going** to meet his parents today.

  He **is not going** to meet his parents today.

  Will or *be going* are often used to predict events or outcomes.

  Example: Bill Clinton **will** be the next President of USA.

  It **is going** to rain heavily this year.

- Simple future tense is not used with time clauses, that is clauses beginning with *when, while, after, before, unless* etc.

  Example: When you will arrive tonight, I will cut the cake. (Incorrect)

  When you arrive tonight, I will cut the cake. (Correct)

- Use in Active/Passive Forms:

  Examples: I will cook the dinner at 7:00 p.m. (Active)

  The dinner will be cooked at 7:00 p.m. (Passive)

<u>**Future Continuous Tense**</u> follows the pattern will be + present participle or am/is/are+going to be + present participle.

Examples: I **will be waiting** for you at the airport.

Will he **be waiting** for you at the airport?

She **is going to be waiting** for you at the airport.

She **is not going to be waiting** for you at the airport.

Different Uses:

- Future Continuous tense is used to indicate that a longer action in the future will be interrupted by a shorter action in the future.

  Examples: I **will be waiting** for you at the airport when your plane lands.

  She **will be watching** the concert tomorrow when you arrive, so she will not meet you tonight.

- It can also be used to indicate a specific time of interruption.

  Examples: Tonight at 8:00 p.m., she **will be watching** the concert.

  At 11:00 a.m. tomorrow morning, we **will be reac*hing*** Hongkong.

In these sentences, it is important to notice that while in Simple Future, a specific time is used to show the time an action will begin or end. In the Future Continuous, a specific time interrupts the action.

- Future continuous may be used to describe parallel actions that are happening at the same time together.

  Examples: I am **going to be working** and he is **going to be watching** a movie.

  After I reach home, I **will be cleaning** up the kitchen, **washing** the utensils and **cooking** food.

- This tense form is also used with a series of parallel actions to create the atmosphere.

  Examples: When I reach home from work, guests **are going to be** at our place. They **will be celebrating** and **are going** *to* have a great time.

- Non-continuous verbs or certain non-continuous uses of mixed verbs cannot be used with future continuous.

  Examples: The guests **will be being** at my house when I arrive. (Incorrect)

  The guests **will be** at my house when I arrive. (Correct)

- Use in Active/Passive Forms:

  Examples: After I reach home tonight, I will be washing the utensils. (Active)

  After I reach home tonight, the utensils are going to be washed by me. (Passive)

Future Perfect has two forms: will have + past participle and am/are/is + going to have + past participle.

Examples:

You **will have perfected** your English by the time you finish this course.

You **will not have perfected** your English unless you study hard.

She is **going to have received** this award by the time I come back.

Are you **going to have received** this award by the time I come back?

Different Uses:

- Future Perfect Tense expresses the idea that something will occur before another action in the future. It can also be used to show that something will happen before a specific time in the future.

  Examples: By this month, I **will have completed** this work.

  She is **going to have received** this award by the time I come back.

- Future Perfect is used with non-continuous verbs and some non-continuous uses of mixed verbs to show that something will continue up until another action in the future.

  Examples: I **will have been** in Paris for two weeks when my boss will arrive.

  By this month end, I **am going to have finished** writing this book.

- This tense form cannot be used with time clauses, such as *when, while, before*, *after* etc.

  Examples: I am going to learn swimming after I will have finished learning yoga. (Incorrect)

  I am going to learn swimming after I have finished learning yoga. (Correct/Passive Forms:

  Examples: He **will have finished** his homework before the teacher asks for it. (Active)

  His homework **will have been finished** before the teacher asks for it. (Passive)

Future Perfect Continuous has two forms: will have been + present participle and am/is/are + going to have been + present participle.

Examples:

The child **will have been sleeping** for over two hours when the father gets back from work.

The child is **going to have been sleeping** when the father gets back home from work.

The child **is not going to have been sleeping** when the father gets back home from work.

Different Uses:

- It is used to show that something will continue up until a particular event or time in the future.

  Examples: The child **will have been sleeping** by the time his father gets back home.

  He is **going to have been working** with us for five years when he leaves for the US to start an independent business.

  How long **will he have been working** with us before he leaves for the US?

- Future perfect continuous is used before another action in the future to show cause and effect.

  Examples: James will be sleeping when you get home because **he will have been suffering** from fever for two days.

  Britney will have lost much weight by now because she is **going to have been dieting** for three months.

- This verb form cannot be used with non-continuous verbs and with some non-continuous uses of mixed verbs.

  Examples: **I will have be having** this tile for over a year. (In correct)

  I will have had this title for over a year. (Correct)

- Like other future tense forms, this tense form cannot be used with time clauses.

  Examples: Tim will not get his promotion unless **he will have been working** hard. (Incorrect)

  Tim will not get his promotion unless he **has been working** hard. (Correct)

■

LESSON 11

Articles and Determiners

Articles

A, an and *the* are referred to as articles. These are demonstrative adjectives.

Kinds of Articles: There are two kinds of articles.

Indefinite Article: *a* and *an* are indefinite articles because these do not refer to a particular or specific person, place or thing.

Definite Article: *the* is a definite article because it is used to refer to a particular person, place or thing.

Examples: David is **a** football player.

This is **an** interesting game.

The boy with blue eyes stood first in the class.

These articles are also known as noun markers or determiners because a noun invariably follows them.

Uses of *A* and *An*:

- These indefinite articles are used to refer to singular nouns.

  Examples: I am eating **an** apple.

  What **a** beautiful picture!

- *An* is used for words that begin with vowels, like *a, e, i, o, u*.

  Examples: She is **an** intelligent student.

  Can you pass me **an** orange?

- *An* is also used for words that begin with vowel like sounds.

  Examples: He is **an** honest man.

  I will be back in **an** hour.

- In certain words that begin with *u* is pronounced as *yoo*. For such words, even though they begin with a vowel, *a* is used.

  Examples: Italy is **a** European country.

  A screwdriver is **a** useful device.

  This is **a** united decision.

- Some words that begin with *o* have a *w* sound. For such words, the article *a* is used.

  Examples: This is just **a** one-time thing.

- Indefinite articles are used when we first refer to something. However, the subsequent references will use the definite article.

  Example: I saw **a** man coming towards me. **The** man looked scary and I was frightened.

  In this sentence, *a* is used when we first refer to the man and when this same man is being referred to the second time, *the* is used because we are referring to a particular and definite person.

- Some times, a modifier may appear between the article and the noun, in such cases, the indefinite article will continue to be used.

  Example: "I want **a** large glass of juice", said Jamie.

  "I have put **a** large glass of juice already", said the bartender.

Uses of *the*:

- *The* is used to refer to definite persons, places or things.

  Examples: **The** earth is one of **the** nine planets that revolve around **the** sun.

  The sun rises in **the** east and sets in **the** west.

- *The* is used to refer to certain proper nouns that are commonly used as common nouns.

  Examples: Kalidas is the Shakespeare of India.

- *The* is also used when the noun refers to something in the abstract.

  Examples: **The** United States has encouraged **the** people to use **the** public transportation system.

- Often in a written text, when subsequent references are made to a person, place or thing, *the* is used.

  Examples: A newspaper serves as the mouthpiece of the people. Often people in a democracy use **the** newspaper to voice their opinion.

- *The* is used to refer to adjectives in the comparative and superlative degree.

  Examples: She is **the** wiser of the two.

  This is **the** most entertaining movie I have ever seen.

- *The* is also used to refer to certain kinds of proper nouns,

  Examples:

- for the names of rivers: the Thames, the Ganga, the Niagra Falls.
- for geographical places: the Sahara Desert, the Thar Desert, the Pacific Ocean, the East, the West, the Western countries, etc.
- for pluralized names, such as family names or names of teams and geographical places: the Netherlands, the Jones, the Bahamas, the West Indies, the American baseball team, the Indian football team etc.
- for public institutions: the Inter-Continental, the Young Men's Cultural Association, the Oxford University, the Roman Catholic Church, etc.

- for names of the newspapers: the New York Times, the Times, etc.
- for nouns followed by prepositional phrases beginning with *of*: the Prime Minister of our country, the Managing Director of the Company, the Head of the Department, etc.
- for names of communities: the Christians, the Muslims, the Islamic people, etc.
- for wars, battles or mutinies: the Second World war, the Mutiny of 1857.

Other Uses of Articles:

- Articles are used for abstract nouns in some cases.

  Examples: The war upset **the** peace of mind of people.

  His mind was upset with grief. It was **a** grief that he had never known before.

- Certain nouns do not use articles, but there are some which have the use of articles.

  Examples:

  - Names of languages: Chinese, French, and English, etc.
  - Used with names of sports and academic subjects: football, basketball, mathematics, science, etc.
  - Used with non-count nouns: wine, dinner, lunch, etc.
  - For generic nouns: the computers, the people.

Determiners

Definition: Determiners are words that modify the nouns with which they are used in some manner or the other. These are used to mark nouns and are also followed by nouns.

Examples: She wants to be **a** doctor.

This apple is rotten.

He has **little** knowledge about the product.

Every one was given a box of chocolates.

Thus, we notice that each determiner in the above-mentioned sentences precedes a noun.

Kinds of Determiners:

- Article Determiners: a, an and the.
- Possessive Nouns: Sam's, my cousin's.
- Demonstratives: this, that, these, those, such.
- Possessive Pronouns: his, her, mine, yours, their, etc.
- Numeral Determiners: those that represent numbers, like one, ten, five, etc.
- Indefinite Pronouns: few, more, many, several, some, etc.

Uses of Determiners:

- For the uses of articles, refer the above section on articles.
- Possessive nouns and pronouns are used to indicate possession: for details refer chapter on nouns and pronouns.
- Demonstrative adjectives and nouns are used to refer to particular object/s. See demonstrative adjectives in chapter on adjectives for further information.
- Possessive pronouns are used to indicate possession. Details discussed in chapter on nouns and pronouns.
- Numeral determiners are used to refer to numeral adjectives that may be either definite (like one, two, etc.) or indefinite, (like some, many, few, several, etc.) or distributive (like each, every, either, neither).

Let us look at the following sentences that consist of different types of determiners.

An apple **a** day keeps the doctor away. (Indefinite Articles)

The Thames River flows through London. (Definite Article)

Give me **Sam's** book. (Possessive noun)

Look at **my cousin's** wardrobe. (Possessive noun)

This is the way towards the London Bridge. (Demonstrative determiner)

Those are the boys who always trouble me. (Demonstrative determiner)

The pink dress is **mine.** (Possessive pronoun)

The huge house at the end of the road is **his**. (Possessive pronoun)

Can I get **two** pencils? (Numeral adjective determiner)

Only a **few** students turned up for the lecture. (Indefinite adjective determiner)

Each one of you is equally naughty. (Distributive adjective determiner)

Related to articles and determiners is another concept of quantifiers. Let us briefly understand what are quantifiers and what function they are used to perform.

Quantifiers

Similar to articles, quantifiers are words that are invariably followed by nouns and are used to modify them. They answer the question how many or how much.

We learnt in the chapter on nouns that nouns may be classified and into count nouns and non-count nouns. Let us now look at which quantifiers are used with count nouns and which are used for non-count nouns.

- The quantifiers that work with count nouns are *many, few, a few, several, couple* and *none*. Let us take the example of the noun *girls* to understand this clearly.

  There were **many** girls standing there.

There were **few** girls there.

Only **a few** of the girls were standing there.

A couple of girls were standing there.

Several girls were standing there.

None of the girls was standing there.

- There are some quantifiers that are used along with non-count nouns. These are *not much, a little, little, bit, a great deal of, a good deal of* and *no*. Let us understand this with the example of the non-count noun *water.*

There is **not much** water left.

There is **little** water.

Only **a little** water is left.

I have **a bit** of water.

I was thirsty and I drank **a good deal of** water.

I was thirsty and I finished **a great deal** of the water that was available.

There is **no** water left.

- Some quantifiers can work with count as well as non-count nouns, such as *all of the, some, most, lack of, lots of, plenty of, enough, a lot.* **Examples**:

All of the girls/water

Some of the girls/water

Most of girls/water

Lack of girls/water

Lots of girls/water

Plenty of girls/water

Enough girls/water

A lot of girls/water

Some other quantifiers: are many, most, much.

- *Much* is used for questions and negative statements.

  Examples: **Much** of the water has already been wasted.

  How **much** money do you have?

  Not **much.**

- *Many:* Some times, indefinite articles are used along with *many*, which then takes a singular verb.

  Examples: *Many a young life* has been wasted in this fiasco.

  Many an orange has ripened by beginning of winters.

- *Most* is some times used with the definite article *the*, as in *most of the*. This quantifier *most of the* may be used with count as well as non-count nouns.

  Examples: **Most of the** students had left by the time the teacher arrived in the class.

  Most of the wine has already been finished.

In the first sentence, the quantifier is used for count noun, *students*, while in the second sentence, it is used for the non-count noun, *wine*.

■

Lesson 12

Modals

Definition: Modal verbs are special verbs, which behave very differently from normal verbs. Some examples are *shall, should, will, would, can, could, must, may, might, ought to.*

Properties of Modals:

- Modal verbs do not take "-s" in the third person.

  Examples: She shoulds be there on time. (Incorrect)

  She should be there on time. (Correct)

  He oughts to be there. (Incorrect)

  He ought to be there. (Correct)

- "not" is used to make modal verbs negative, even in Simple Present and Simple Past.

  Examples: He could not come here.

  She may not come.

- Many modal verbs cannot be used in the past tenses or the future tenses.

  Examples: She will do this work. (Incorrect)

  She will do this work. (Correct)

  He ought to came. (Incorrect)

  He ought to come. (Correct)

Now, let us understand the uses of these modals.

Uses of *Shall*:

a) Used with a subject in first person to refer to simple future.

Examples: I **shall** see you tomorrow.

We **shall** leave for Venice tonight

b) Used with first person in a question to understand what the other person desires?

Examples: **Shall** I make you a cup of coffee?

Shall I help you finish this?

c) Used with subjects in second and third person as a command, promise or threat.

Examples: The teacher told the student, " You **shall** finish this assignment now."

You **shall** be punished for this mistake.

Uses of *Should*: Should is the past form of shall.

a) Used to denote future tense.

Examples: He said that I **should** report for duty on Tuesday.

She insisted that he **should** attend her wedding.

b) Used to refer to a duty or obligation.

Examples: The servant **should** clean the house.

We **should** help the unfortunate.

c) Used for advice, suggestion.

Examples: He **should** work hard if he wants to pass the annual examination.

We **should** listen to our elders.

d) Used to indicate suppositions or assumptions.

Examples: **Should** you need any help, I am always there.

Uses of *Will*:

a) Used with subjects in second and third person to refer to simple future tense.

Examples: He **will** leave for India today.

She **will** turn fifteen this year.

b) Used with subjects in first person as a certainty, promise or willingness.

Examples: I **will** help you solve this case.

We **will** co-operate with the new teacher.

c) Used with first person subjects as a threat or determination.

Examples: I **will** become a famous lawyer one day. (Determination)

I **will** see what they can do. (Threat)

Uses of *Would*:

a) Used in indirect speech to talk about a thing or event of future tense in the past.

Examples: He said that he **would** also join us for lunch.

I told him that I **would** help him.

b) Used to indicate a past habit.

Examples: He **would** go for swimming after work.

He **would** smoke before eating anything.

c) Used in the interrogative to make a request.

Examples: **Would** you pass me a glass of water?

Would you help me unlock this door?

d) Used to wish for unreal situations.

Examples: **Would** that I was young again!

Uses of *Can*:

a) Used to indicate a person's ability to do something.

Examples: I **can** climb up the stairs very fast.

She **can** sing beautifully.

b) Used to indicate a possibility.

Examples: Any one **can** do this.

Every one **can** make mistakes.

c) Used to ask permission for something.

Examples: **Can** I watch a movie with you?

Can you drop me to work today?

d) Used to permit an action.

Examples: You **can** pick any card.

You **cannot** waste your precious time like this.

Uses of *Could*:

a) Used in the past tense to refer to a person's ability to do something.

Examples: She **could** sing beautifully as a child.

She asked me if I **could** help her finish her work.

b) Used in the past tense to indicate a possibility.

Examples: If he had more money, he **could** buy a sports car.

If she had won the elections, she **could** have become a cabinet minister.

Uses of *May*:

a) Used to ask for permission.

Examples: **May** I come in?

May I use your computer?

b) Used to give permission.

Examples: You **may** come in.

You **may** use my computer.

c) Used to indicate a possibility.

Examples: It **may** rain in the evening.

We **may** go out for a movie today.

d) Used to indicate a purpose.

Examples: I am earning so that I **may** be able to complete my studies.

Tom is living with his friend so that he **may** be able to save some money to send to his poor parents.

e) Used to indicate a wish.

Examples: **May** you live a hundred years!

May God shower all His blessings on you!

Uses of *Might*: Might is the past tense of may.

a) Used to indicate a purpose in past tense.

Examples: He saved some money every month so that he **might** be able to donate it to charity.

She wore new clothes so that she **might** look beautiful.

b) Used in the past tense to indicate a possibility.

Examples: It is a sunny day, but it just **might** rain.

James has not come till now, but he **might** turn up.

He said that I **might** get elected.

c) Used to indicate permission in past tense.

Examples: The teacher told the students that they **might** put their heads down if they want to.

The coach said that the players **might** take rest if they were feeling tired.

Uses of *Must:*

a) Used to indicate necessity or obligation.

Examples: His father told him, "You **must** clear all your debts at once."

We **must** respect our elders.

b) Used to indicate compulsion.

Examples: No appointments **must** be made without the

consent of the Chairman of the company.

You **must** come to work on time.

c) Used to offer emphatic advice.

I think you **must** tell the truth.

All students **must** attend their classes regularly.

d) Used to express a belief or opinion with certainty.

Examples: He **must** be turning fifty this year.

This **must** be a poor family.

e) Used to prohibit some action.

Examples: You **must** not go out without asking your mother.

He **must** not show his face to me ever again.

Uses of *Ought to*:

Ought to is used to express a social or a moral obligation.

Examples: We **ought to** serve our country with a sense of pride.

You **ought to** stand by your aging parents.

We **ought to** respect and obey our parents.

■

LESSON 13

Voice and Narration

Voice

Voice is the property of a verb that is used to show whether the subject is performing the action or experiencing it.

Examples:

Belinda likes David.

David is liked by Belinda.

The first sentence shows the subject *Belinda* experiencing the act of liking *David*. The second sentence shows the subject, *David* experiencing the liking of *Belinda*.

Types of Voice: There are two types of voice: active voice and passive voice.

- **Active Voice**: If the subject of the sentence is performing an act on his/her own, it is known as active voice.

  Examples: He crossed the road.

  She lights the candle.

  In these sentences, the subjects *he* in the first sentence and *she* in the second are performing their respective actions and thus these are sentences in active voice.

- **Passive Voice**: If an act is being performed for the subject of the sentence, it is referred to as passive voice.

  Examples: The road was crossed by him.

The candle is lighted by her.

In the above sentences, *the road* and *the candle* are the subjects for whom the acts are being performed. In the first sentence, the subject *road* was crossed by him and in the second sentence, the subject, *the candle* is lighted by her.

Rules to Change Active Voice to Passive: The following rules must be kept in mind while changing the voice from active to passive.

a) The subject gets changed to the object and vice versa.

   Example: Sam is reading a book (Active)

   A book is being read by Sam. (Passive)

   Notice, how in the above sentence, a change of voice leads to a change of the subject and the object of the sentence. In the active voice, *Sam* is the subject and *a book* is the object. When this sentence is changed to the passive, *a book* becomes the new subject and *Sam* becomes the new object.

b) The new object is preceded by *by*.

   Taking the above example again, the new object, *Sam* is preceded by *by*.

c) Stick to the tense form given. Do not change the tense while changing the voice.

   Looking at the same example, we observe that while changing the voice, the tense form remains unaltered; we do not change the present tense to past or future tense.

d) While changing from active to passive, some pronouns that may be used as the objects of the sentence get changed as follows:

Existing Pronoun	**Changed Pronoun**
Me	I
You	you
Her	she

Them	they
Us	we
Him	he.

It remains *it* and whom gets replaced by *who*.

Let us look at some more examples to understand the rules for this change more clearly:

- Does she pluck flowers? (Active)
  Are flowers plucked by her? (Passive)
- He tells lies. (Active)
  Lies are told by him. (Passive)
- My parents expect good news. (Active)
  Good news is expected by my parents. (Passive)
- He has written this book. (Active)
  This book has been written by him. (Passive)

In these sentences, we notice that the subject of the sentence in active voice changes to the object of the sentence when re-written in passive voice. For example, in the first sentence, the subject *she* becomes the object and the object *flowers* change to the subject, when the sentence is converted from active to passive voice. The pronoun *she* gets replaced by *her* and the sentence retains its tense form.

Changing Voice in Imperative Sentences:

Let us now look at some imperative sentences and how they are changed in to passive voice.

Active Voice	Passive Voice
Shut the door.	Let the door be shut.
Post the letter at once.	Let the letter be posted at once.
Always speak the truth.	Let the truth be spoken always.

Please do me a favour.	You are requested to do me a favour.
Get out of my way.	You are ordered to get out of my way.

The first three sentences begin with *let* and the nouns in these sentences are preceded by *be/not be.*

Sentences which indicate a request, such those beginning with *kindly* or *please*, when changed to passive, the request *kindly* or *please*, gets changed to *requested*. In sentences like the last sentence, where orders or commands are given, the passive form includes the word *ordered* or *commanded*.

Sentences Using Infinite Verbs:

Active Voice	**Passive Voice**
You ought to do your duty.	Your duty ought to be done.
There is no house to let.	There is no house to be let.
I hope to finish the work on time.	I hope the work to be finished on time.

Thus, we notice that in case of sentences using infinitives, a change to passive voice involves the use of to + be + verb.

In some cases, we may come across sentences that use two objects. In such instances, the object closest to the verb gets changed into subject of the sentence in passive voice.

Examples: The Principal refused the boys admission. (Active)

The boys were refused admission by the Principal. (Passive)

Or Admission was refused to the boys by the Principal. (Passive)

This teacher teaches us Mathematics. (Active)

We are taught Mathematics by this teacher. (Passive)

Or Mathematics is taught to us by this teacher. (Passive)

Sentences Using Prepositions:

In sentences, where there is a preposition linked to a verb of a sentence in active form, the passive form of the sentence shall follow the pattern new subject + is/was/will be + past participle of the verb + preposition + by + new object.

Let us look at some examples to understand this clearly.

He laughed at the old beggar. (Active)

The old beggar was laughed at by him. (Passive)

She will definitely look into this matter. (Active)

This matter will be definitely looked into by her. (Passive)

In the first sentence, *he* is the subject, *the old beggar* is the object, *laughed* is the verb and *at* is the preposition. The change to passive form, changes the subject to *the old beggar, he* becomes the object. Following the pattern indicated above, the sentence looks like:

The old beggar (new subject) + was + laughed (past participle of the verb) + at (preposition) + by + him (new object).

Narration

Definition: The art of reporting the words of the speaker, without altering the meaning of the sentence, is known as narration.

Examples:

Roger said to his mother, " I will be late today."

In this example, we notice that the speaker, Roger's words are quoted as spoken by him. This fact is elucidated by the use of inverted commas to report what Roger said to his mother. " I will be late today" is known as reported speech. Such a narration is referred to as direct speech or direct narration.

Now, let us see that if we were to report what Roger said, without quoting his words and without altering the meaning of the sentence, what the same sentence would look like.

Roger told his mother that he would be late that day.

This altered sentence conveys the complete meaning of what Roger said to his mother, in our own words. Such a narration is known as indirect speech or indirect narration.

Kinds of Narration:

As we understand from the above example, there are two main kinds of narration: direct speech or narration and indirect speech or narration.

Rules for Changing From Direct to Indirect Speech:

Thus, we notice the following points, which need to be bore in mind while changing the form of narration from direct to indirect:

a. Inverted commas disappear when the sentence is rewritten in indirect speech. In their place, a conjunction *that* is used.

b. *Said to* becomes *told.*

c. The verb *will* changes to its past form *would.*

d. The first person changes to the third person, that is *I* becomes *he*.

e. *Today* gets replaced by *that day*.

Let us follow these rules to change the following sentences to indirect speech.

1) David said to James, " I will leave soon." (Direct)

   David told James that he would leave soon. (Indirect)

2) The teacher said to John, "You must learn to finish your work on time." (Direct)

   The teacher told John that he must learn to finish his wok on time. (Indirect)

Some Important Points:

- The first-person pronouns of the reported speech are changed to third-person pronouns of the indirect speech according to the given subject of the former.

Examples:

1) He said, " I will win the race this year."

He said that he would win the race that year.

2) Julia said, " I am unwell."

Julia said that she was unwell.

- The second-person pronouns of the reported speech get changed according to the object of the direct speech.

Examples:

1) She said to me, "You have done your duty." (Direct)

She told me that I had done my duty. (Indirect)

2) The teacher said to Sam, " If you work hard, you will pass the exam with flying colours." (Direct)

The teacher told Sam that if he worked hard, he would pass the exam with flying colours. (Indirect)

- Third-person pronouns that may appear in reported speech remain unchanged when the narration is changed to indirect.

Examples:

1) She said to her mother, " He does not take coffee." (Direct)

She told her mother that he did not take coffee. (Indirect)

2) Every one says, " They have told a lie."

Every one says that they have told a lie.

- If the reporting verb in the reported speech is in the present or the future tense, its tense remains unchanged, while changing its narration.

Examples:

1) Sally says, " Sam is hitting me." (Direct)

Sally says that Sam is hitting her. (Indirect)

2) Sally will say, " Sam is hitting me." (Direct)

Sally will say that Sam is hitting her. (Indirect)

- If the reporting verb is in the past tense, while changing the narration, the tense of the verb gets changed to past tense.

Examples:

1) She said, " I am flying to Indonesia tomorrow." (Direct)

She said that she was flying to Indonesia the next day. (Indirect)

2) Mr. Bush said, " I am going to the market." (Direct)

Mr. Bush said that he was going to the market. (Indirect)

- If the reported speech reports a universal truth or, a past historical fact or a habitual fact, its tense remains unchanged. The same rule applies if two actions are reported to be happening at the same time.

Examples:

1) The teacher said, " The moon revolves around the earth." (Direct)

The teacher said that the moon revolves around the earth. (Indirect)

2) The mother complained to the father, "Our son still smokes a lot." (Direct)

The mother complained to the father that their son still smokes a lot. (Indirect)

3) The History teacher said, " The Second World War ended with the US dropping the atom bomb on Hiroshima and Nagasaki." (Direct)

The History teacher said that the Second World War ended with the US dropping the atom bomb on Hiroshima and Nagasaki. (Indirect)

- If the reported speech conveys an imagined condition, its tense form remains the same.

Examples: He said, " I wish I were young again." (Direct)

He said that he wished that he were young again. (Indirect)

- If the reported speech consists of the third-person pronoun, to infinitive or modal verbs, there is no change in its tense.

  Examples: The teacher said to the students, "You must obey your elders." (Direct)

  The teacher told the students that they must obey their elders. (Indirect)

- While changing the narration from direct to indirect, some words change as follows:

Direct Narration	**Indirect Narration**
Here	there
Now	then
This	that
These	those
Today	that day
Yesterday	the previous day
Tomorrow	the next day
Next week	the following week
Ago	before
Hence	thence
Thus	so

Changing Narration in Interrogative Sentences:

Let us look at the following examples:

1) She said to the servant, "Is the tea ready for me?" (Direct)

   She asked the servant if the tea was ready for her. (Indirect)

2) The teacher said to the students, "Is the work done?" (Direct)

   The teacher asked the students if the work was done. (Indirect)

Thus, we notice that in interrogative sentences, the reporting verb *said* or *said to* gets changed to *asked*. If the question in the reported speech contains *is, am, are, was, were, do, does, will, may, can* etc., *is, am* etc. gets replaced by *if* or whether.

Changing Narration in Imperative Sentences:

Sentences in which an order, a command, a request or an advice is given are known as imperative sentences. While changing the narration, the reporting verb *said to* gets changed into *requested, ordered, commanded, warned, forbade* or *advised*. Let us look at some examples:

1) The General said to the soldiers, "March forward and defeat the enemy." (Direct)

   The General ordered the soldiers to march forward and defeat the enemy. (Indirect)

2) Charles said to her, "Please pass me a glass of water." (Direct)

   Charles requested her to pass him a glass of water. (Indirect)

3) The doctor said to the patient, "You must take complete rest." (Direct)

   The doctor advised the patient to take complete rest. (Indirect)

4) He said to the girl, " Do not go any further." (Direct)

   He warned the girl not to go any further. (Indirect)

In case of sentences that begin with "let": *let* gets replaced by *suggested* or *proposed*, if it indicates a suggestion or a proposal and if it indicates allowing a permission or persuasion, *said to* gets replaced with *requested* or *ordered*.

1) John said to his younger brothers, "Let us play hide and seek." (Direct)

   John suggested to his younger brothers that they play hide and seek. (Indirect)

2) She said to her boss, "Let me go home early today." (Direct)

   She requested her boss to let her go home early that day. (Indirect)

3) The Headmistress told the girls, " Let the teacher come in my room." (Direct)

   The Headmistress ordered the girls to let the teacher come in her room. (Indirect)

Changing Narration in Exclamatory Sentences:

Let us look at the following sentences:

1) The coach said to his team, "*Alas!* We have lost the match again." (Direct)
2) The coach said to his team, "*Hurrah!* We have won the match." (Direct)
3) He said, "*Sorry!* I cannot come to the party." (Direct)
4) He said to his mother, "*What!* She has got married?" (Direct)

The following exclamatory remarks are changed as follows:

1) The coach *exclaimed with sorrow* that they had lost the match again. (Indirect)
2) The coach *exclaimed with joy* that they had won the match. (Indirect)
3) He *exclaimed with regret* that he could not come to the party. (Indirect)
4) He *exclaimed with surprise* that she had got married. (Indirect)

Miscellaneous Examples:

1) He said, "O that I had the wings of a bird." (Direct)

   This sentence expresses a wish of the speaker and is therefore changed as:

   He wished that he had the wings of a bird. (Indirect)

2) David's grandfather said to him, " May you live a hundred years." (Direct)

   This sentence expresses the prayer of *David's grandfather* and is changed as:

   David's grandfather prayed that he might live a hundred years. (Indirect)

3) The patient said, "Thank you, doctor." (Direct)

   The patient thanked the doctor. (Indirect)

4) The accused said, " Yes, I committed the murder." (Direct)

   The accused admitted that he had committed the murder. (Indirect)

5) The boy said, " Good morning father." (Direct)

   The boy wished his father good morning. (Indirect)

■

Lesson 14

Punctuation

Need to Learn Punctuation

Punctuation is using the right commas, full stops, etc. at the right places. It is everything in written language other than actual words, including punctuation marks, indentation, capitalisation, etc.

You may be wondering what is the need to understand punctuation in order to speak English. We need to know about the usage of punctuation marks so that in our spoken English we can stop at the right places. This is important because a person may be speaking perfect English, without any grammatical errors, but he/she may not be stopping or pausing where required. This can lead to the listener misunderstanding the point of the speaker.

For example, let's look at the following sentence:

Eats shoots and leaves

This sentence is written without any punctuation marks. If we were to rewrite the same sentence using punctuation, it will appear as:

Eats, shoots and leaves.

Even though the actual words are the same in both the sentences, they are poles apart in terms of their meaning. Thus, in English language, an understanding of punctuation is essential to convey to the listener the actual meaning of the sentence and also to comprehend properly the spoken English of others.

Now, that we understand the need to learn and know about punctuation marks, let us look at the various punctuation marks that are used in English language.

Punctuation Marks

First of all it is essential to understand what are punctuation marks. Punctuation marks are symbols in a language that correspond to neither the sounds of the language nor its words and phrases, but which are used to indicate the structure and organisation of writing. The punctuation marks commonly used in English are comma, semi colon, full stop and inverted commas, etc.

Now, let us look at each one of these in detail and understand their uses.

The Comma

- The comma is used in cases where a co-coordinating conjunction links two separate clauses.

  Example: I wore footpads to prevent my heels from hurting, but they still hurt as if I had danced wearing high heels for two days nonstop.

- Comma is used after an introductory adverb clause and many times also after an introductory phrase. If the introductory phrase is short, then the comma may not be used.

  Examples: After the state government had completed its AIDS awareness campaign, a sudden drop in the number of patients suffering from AIDS was reported.

- It is also used to separate items in a series.

  Example: I am carrying scissors, tweezers, a screwdriver and a bottle-opener along with me.

- Used to separate the reporting verb in the reported speech.

  Examples: The shepherd said, "How foolish of me to trust my sheep to a wolf?"

Some Important Points:

- A comma should be never be used to separate the subject of the sentence from its predicate.

  Examples: Registering before the 20th of July for this fitness programme, will entitle you to a good discount. (Incorrect)

  Registering before the 20th of July for this fitness programme will entitle you to a good discount. (Correct)

- It should not be used to separate a verb from its object or subject complement or a preposition from its object.

  Examples: I hope to mail to you before Halloween, a current picture of my new pet chickens. (Incorrect)

  I hope to mail to you before Halloween a current picture of my new pet chickens. (Correct)

- It should not be used after a coordinating conjunction.

  Examples: Scary noises of unnatural movements were heard from the empty house upstairs but, the neighbours were used to it and paid no attention. (Incorrect)

  Scary noises of unnatural movements were heard from the empty house upstairs but the neighbours were used to it and paid no attention. (Incorrect)

- The comma must not be used to set off words and short phrases, especially those that are introductory in nature and are not parenthetical.

  Examples: After lunch, we will learn clay molding. (Incorrect)

  After lunch we will learn clay molding. (Correct)

- It should not be used before the first or the last item of a series.

  Examples: He went to school carrying with him his schoolbag packed with, a pencil box, colour crayons, textbooks and comics. (Incorrect)

He went to school carrying with him his schoolbag packed with a pencil box, colour crayons, textbooks and comics. (Correct)

- Comma should also not be used to set off restrictive elements.

  His thumb, on his left hand, is bigger than that on his right. (Incorrect)

  His thumb on his left hand is bigger than that on his right. (Correct)

Semi-Colon

- Semi-colon is used to link two independent clauses that are not joined together by a coordinating conjunction. However, it should be used to join only those independent clauses that are closely related in meaning.

  Examples: Yogic asanas help to prevent many diseases; a little care is also important.

- A semi-colon should not be used to link a dependent clause or phrase to an independent clause.

  Examples: Although losing weight and maintaining the weight loss, takes a lot of time; the time and effort is well paid for in the long run. (Incorrect)

  Although losing weight and maintaining the weight loss takes a lot of time, the time and effort is well paid for in the long run. (Correct)

- It should not be used before a coordinating conjunction that links two independent clauses.

  Examples: The inflation has been increasing steadily for many years now; but some signs of control are finally beginning to show. (Incorrect)

  The inflation has been increasing steadily for many years now, but some signs of control are finally beginning to show. (Correct)

- An important clue about using semi-colon is that it is often used where you can also use a full stop.
- When punctuating a list or series of elements in which one or more of the elements contains an internal comma, you should use semicolons instead of commas to separate the elements from one another.

  Examples: John's father believes two things; that no situation, however serious, will be happily resolved; the Almight knows best and that when the right time comes, even the toughest of situations will melt away.

Colon

- The colon is used to focus the reader's attention on what is to follow. It is used to introduce a list or an idea that somehow completes the introductory idea. However, a colon may be used in this way only after an independent clause.

  Examples: I visited three cities during my stay in Australia: Cannes, Melbourne and Sydney.

  Her grandmother gave her a good counsel: to stop worrying about things we cannot control and instead, focus on what we can do and how to do it best.
- A colon should not be placed between a verb and its object or its subject complement or between a preposition and its object.

  Examples:

  1) He carried: a pencil box, colour crayons, textbooks and comics with him to school. (Incorrect)

  In this sentence, the colon is wrongly placed between the verb *carried* and the object. This same sentence is written correctly as follows:

  He carried a pencil box, colour crayons, textbooks and comics with him to school. (Correct)

  2) We travelled to: London, New South Wales and Ireland. (Incorrect)

In this sentence, colon is used between preposition to and its object. This same sentence is written correctly as follows:

We travelled to London, New South Wales and Ireland. (Correct)

End Punctuation

The punctuation marks that are used to mark the end of a sentence are referred to as end punctuation. The full stop or period, question mark and exclamation mark are end punctuation marks.

- The **period or full stop** is the most common form of end punctuation. It is used to mark the end of a sentence.

  Examples:

  1) He is a dear friend of mine.

  2) We travelled the whole of Europe within a month.

- It is also used to signal the end of imperative sentences that have no sense of urgency.

  Examples:

  1) Get me a cup of coffee.

  2) Take a left and then a right turn.

- The **exclamation mark** is used to end imperative sentences that convey a strong feeling or a sense of urgency.

  Examples:

  1) Look below!

  2) Shut up!

  3) Oouch! That hurts.

- The **question mark** is used to signal the end of a direct question.

  Examples:

  1) Whose house is this?

  2) Why do you come so late to class?

  3) What are you doing here?

Quotation Marks

- Quotation marks are used to mark quoted material or speech. In such cases, double quotation marks are placed both before and after the quoted text.

  Examples: She said to me, "Will you join me for a cup of coffee?"

  It is rightly said, "Laughter is the best medicine."

- Quotation marks are also used to mark title of short works such as short stories, essays or poems, etc.

  Examples: I read "The New York Times" every morning.

  "The Little Black Boy" is an informative poem that conveys the message that in God's kingdom, there are no differences between a white child and a black child.

  In such cases single inverted commas may also be used.

- Occasionally, quotation marks are also used to point out certain words.

  Examples: I think you have used the word "incredible" many times in this essay.

  The word "inevitable" means something that is certain and cannot be avoided or escaped.

  Here also single inverted commas may be used. And, if a quotation comes within a quoted material, that may also be marked with single inverted commas.

How to Use Other Punctuation Marks With Quotation Marks:

A lot of people often wonder how to use other punctuation marks along with quotation marks. The following tips should prove handy:

- **Commas and Full Stops**: these come in within the quotation marks.

  Examples: She said to me, " Will you give me company?"

Henry said, " I have travelled to Egypt, Italy, France, Greece and Indonesia."

- **Semi-Colons and Colons**: these always go outside the quotation marks.

  Examples: The students really liked the poem "The Little Black Boy"; in fact, it was one of their favourite poems.

  Blake clearly states his opinion in his poem "The Little Black Boy": he believes there are no distinctions between black and white people in the eyes of God.

- **Question Marks, Exclamations and Hyphens**: these go within the quotation marks, if they are a part of the quotation and are placed outside if not so.

  Examples: The teacher asked James, "Where is your homework?"

  He said, "What! She is getting married to you?"

Apostrophe

- An apostrophe is used to indicate the possessive case of a noun.

  Examples: This book that you are reading is Carol's.

  I will see you at Henry's bar.

  The apostrophe in these sentences is used to indicate possession, *Carol's* and *Henry's*.

- Apostrophe is also used when letters are deliberately left out in contraction.

  Examples: I haven't read a book for ages.

  She didn't do her work.

  Here, the apostrophe is being used for contractions, such as *haven't* is a contraction for have not and *didn't* is a contraction for did not.

- In case of plural nouns, the apostrophe is placed after the *s* to indicate possession.

Examples: This is a ladies' washroom.

His daughters' security was his greatest worry.

- Possessive pronouns such as *his, yours, theirs, its* and *hers* do not take apostrophes.

Examples: The truck bumped into the car and damaged its bumper.

This house is hers.

Theirs is the grandest bungalow I have ever seen.

Dash or Hyphen

- A dash, also known as a hyphen, may be used at the beginning and end of parenthetical information. Hyphens may be used in case the parenthetical information is too long or abrupt to set off with commas.

Examples: She looked splendid wearing her blue evening gown in silk- the one that has been personally designed by a famous dress designer.

The idea of doing away with examinations up to primary school level- that has many teachers and educational heads supporting it- has finally obtained the nod from the Department of Education as well.

- A hyphen may be used to conclude a list of elements, focusing them all towards one point.

Examples: Proteins, vitamins and iron- all can be found in this nutritious dish.

- It is also used to mark sharp turns in thoughts.

Examples: We went through proposals from Baskin Robbins, Gelatto- The Diet Ice-cream and two other ice-cream vendors- and turned them all down.

In all the examples given above, a dash may also be used in order to distance out the matter in between, or that follows.

■

Lesson 15

Building Phrases

A phrase may be defined as a group of two or more grammatically linked words without a subject and a predicate.

Examples:

both the employer and the employees.

In the night sky.

In these examples, we notice that each word is linked grammatically to the other and forms a group known as a phrase on its own, without an associated subject and a predicate. A phrase is often used to add information to an already existing sentence and it may function as a subject, object, verb, adjective, adverb, a subject complement or an object complement.

Examples:

We saw lightning flash **in the night sky**.

Both the employer and the employees worked together to meet the deadline.

Small children get a thrill out of doing things on their own.

Function of Phrases:

A phrase may function as a noun, adjective, verb or adverb.

Noun Phrases:

A noun phrase contains a noun or a pronoun with any of the associated modifiers. It may function as a subject, the object of a verb or verbal, as an object of preposition or as a subject or object complement.

Examples:

Small children get a thrill out of doing things on their own. (Used as a subject)

To teach the students to read, speak and write correctly is **the teacher's aim**. (Used as an object of a verb)

The thieves were caught red-handed **by a smart boy**. (Object of a preposition)

Shakespeare is the name of a famous dramatist, **not an athlete**. (Used as a subject complement)

I like to play with **small children**. (Used as an object complement)

Some verbals, such as gerunds and infinitives can act as nouns and thus form the nucleus of many noun phrases.

Examples:

Ice-skating is a popular activity in the hilly areas.

I am planning **to prepay the loan** and free my house from the mortgage.

Adjective Phrases:

An adjective phrase is one that modifies a noun or a pronoun. Participles or prepositions along with their objects are used to form adjective phrases.

Examples:

I was unable to study due to the noise **of my neighbour's nonstop dance party.**

In this sentence, the phrase **of my neighbour's nonstop dance party** is a prepositional phrase that acts as an adjective modifying the noun **noise**.

Our company supports the children **orphaned in the 9/11 disaster.**

In the above sentence, the participle phrase **orphaned in the 9/11 disaster** acts as an adjective modifying the noun **children.**

Verb Phrases:

A verb phrase contains a verb, its objects and any adverbs, adverb phrases and adverb clauses that function to modify it. A sentence's or a clause's predicate is always a verb phrase.

Examples:

Jade is **trying to decide whether she wants to become a doctor or wants to pursue a law course.**

I did not have all the ingredients that were required to make the chocolate cake.

After he **started working**, Joseph **felt more independent**.

Adverb Phrase:

A prepositional phrase can also be an adverb phrase, functioning as an adverb.

Examples:

Mother bought some vegetables when she went **to the grocery store**.

In this sentence, the prepositional phrase **to the grocery store** functions as an adverb modifying the verb **went**.

We saw the lightning flash **in the night sky**.

In this sentence, the prepositional phrase **in the night sky** acts as an adverb phrase modifying the verb **flash**.

We will meet in the conference room for a meeting **at 4:00 p.m.**

In this sentence, the prepositional phrase **at 4:00 p.m.**, acts as an adverb modifying the verb phrase **will meet**.

■

LESSON 16

Clauses

A clause may be defined as a group of grammatically linked words including a subject and a predicate. Clauses are like the building blocks of sentences. Each sentence contains at least one clause.

It is important to understand the difference between clauses and phrases. Whereas a phrase contains no subject and predicate, a clause contains a subject or a predicate or both. Let us attempt to understand this distinction with the help of some examples:

1) Monkeys eat bananas.

   This sentence contains a subject, *monkeys* and a predicate *eat bananas*. Thus, it is an example of a clause.

2) Monkeys eating bananas.

   This sentence is an example of a noun phrase. Although, it may function as a subject, but there is no predicate following it.

3) Monkeys eating bananas are a common sight on this road.

   This sentence too, like the first sentence, makes complete sense and is a clause. It has a subject *monkeys eating bananas* and *are a common sight on this road* is the predicate.

4) Run!

   This one-word command is also a clause. It makes complete sense and there is a definite person to whom the speaker is giving this command.

Kinds of Clauses:

Clauses may be either dependent or independent.

Independent Clauses: Some clauses can stand alone as sentences and are referred to as independent clauses.

Examples:

the President is the head of the state

the President is in Italy

Dependent Clauses: are those clauses that cannot stand independently as sentences.

Examples:

because the President is the head of the state

when the President is in Italy

These sentences cannot function independently. They require the assistance of other words or clauses in order to convey complete sense. The dependent clauses are also known as subordinating clauses.

Such sentences may function as nouns, adjectives or adverbs in a sentence.

Noun Clause:

A noun clause is a clause that takes the place of a noun. A noun clause may act as a subject or object of a verb or an object of preposition.

Examples:

He told me **that he was feeling unwell.**

Here, the noun clause answers the question *what did he tell you?*

That she would come is doubtful.

In this sentence, the noun clause answers the question *what is doubtful*?

Noun clause as subject to a verb:

Examples:

When he will return is uncertain.

In this sentence, the noun clause answers the question *when will he return*?

What he said is wrong.

Here, the noun clause answers the question *what is wrong*?

Noun clause as an object to a verb:

Examples:

I cannot say **what he wants**.

In this sentence, the noun clause answers the question *what can you not say*?

Do you know **when the train will arrive**?

Thus, we notice that noun clauses functioning as subjects or objects of verbs in sentences, answer questions such as *who, what, when, whom, why how, whose,* etc.

Noun clause as an object to a preposition:

Examples:

Please listen to **what I say**.

Your success will depend on **how you work**.

Adjective Clause

An adjective clause is a subordinating clause that takes the place of an adjective in a phrase or another clause. It modifies a noun or a pronoun and answers the questions *which* or *what kind of*?

Examples:

He is the boy **who hurt that child**.

In this sentence, the adjective clause modifies the noun *boy* and follows the noun that it modifies.

In formal writing, the adjective clause often begins with relative pronouns *whom, that, which, who, whose.* Let us now look at some examples using relative pronouns.

Examples:

This is the book **that I read**.

The fish **that he ate** was delicious.

I have lost the book **which you gave me**.

Where is the man **whom you called**?

The cops are searching for the thief **who stole her necklace**.

Adverb Clause

An adverb clause functions as an adverb in a phrase or another clause. It often answers the questions *when, where, why, under what conditions* and *with what result*?

Examples:

The Chairman gave a speech **where the workers were working.**

In this sentence, the adverb clause answers the question *where*?

If he works hard, he will pass.

Here, the adverb clause answers the question *under what condition will he pass*?

After Jennifer eloped with her boyfriend, her father did not wish to see her face again.

This is an example of adverb clause of time and answers the question *when did her father not wish to see her face again?*

She wanted to start working **so that she could support her family**.

This is an example of an adverb clause of effect. It answers the question *why did she want to start working?*

She started working **because she had to support her family**.

This sentence is an example of an adverb clause of cause and like the previous example answers the question *why?*

■

LESSON 17

Sentence Formation and Kinds of Sentences

Sentence Formation

A sentence is a group of words which put together convey complete meaning and sense. Let us look at some sample sentences.

Examples: A famous artist is going to paint the picture.

Susan is playing piano.

When I reached home, the guests had already arrived.

If you look carefully, you will observe that these sentences have two parts or components. The first part is the subject of the sentence about whom the rest of the sentence gives further information. The further information that is provided by the rest of the sentence is referred to as the predicate.

Let us look at the first sentence:

A famous artist *is going to paint the picture*.

The first half of the sentence, *a famous artist*, which has been underlined, is the subject of the sentence. The second part, *is going to paint the picture*, is the predicate that gives us further information about the artist. This sentence like all other sentences contains a verb, which in this case is *going*.

Some Important Points:

- When the subject of a sentence consists of two or more nouns or pronouns, connected by *and,* a plural verb is used.

  Examples: He and his friends are watching a movie together.

  Roger and James are good friends.

  The subject in the first sentence consists of two pronouns and in the second sentence it consists of two nouns, joined together by **and**, taking the plural verb **are**.

- In cases where two or more nouns or pronouns are joined together by *nor* or *or*, a singular verb is used.

  Examples: You may come alone or bring along a companion.

- If the compound subject of a sentence consists of a combination of singular or plural nouns, or pronouns, joined by *or* or *nor*, the verb should be in consonance with the part of the subject that is closer to the verb.

  Examples: Neither she nor her friends came to the party.

  Her friends and the lady jog every day in the park.

  In the first sentence, the plural pronoun *friends* is closer to the verb *came*. Accordingly the verb is in consonance with the plural pronoun. Similarly, in the second sentence, the singular noun *lady* is closer to the verb *jog* and the two are in consonance with each other.

- Some times, phrases come in between the subject and the verb. In such instances, the verb should be in agreement with the subject and not the noun or pronoun of the phrase.

  Example: The persons who prefer that kind of music are very few.

  Charles as well as his football team is anxious about the outcome of the match.

  In the first sentence, the verb *are* is in agreement with the subject *the persons* and not influenced by the phrase *who prefer that kind of music*.

- *Doesn't* is a contracted form of *does not* and should be always used with singular subject. *Don't* is a contraction of *do not* and must be used with plural nouns or first person and second person pronouns such as *I* and *you*.

  Examples: He doesn't come here.

  She doesn't come here.

  I don't come here.

  You don't come here.

- Some nouns like *news, mathematics, civics, measles* and *dollars* need singular verbs.

  Examples: Ten dollars is a lot of money for such a poor person.

  News will be telecast at 8:00 p.m.

  Mathematics is a difficult subject.

- The words *each*, *each one*, *either*, *neither*, *everyone*, *everybody*, *anybody*, *anyone*, *nobody*, *somebody*, *someone*, and *no one* are singular and require a singular verb.

  Examples: Each one of you is responsible for this failure.

  Neither John nor James has passed the test.

  Will someone tell me where is the rest of the class?

- Nouns such as *scissors*, *tweezers*, *trousers*, and *shears* require plural verbs.

  Examples: Can you pass me a pair of scissors?

  Tweezers are useful and handy.

- Usually, for collective nouns, a singular verb is used.

  Examples: I saw a flock of cows at the sideway.

  The entire team is responsible for its outstanding performance in the World Cup.

- In sentences that begin with *there is* or *there are*, as there is no subject, the verb should agree with the following part of the sentence.

  Examples: There is no body who can answer this question?

  There are many questions to answer.

- Expressions such as *with*, *together with*, *including*, *accompanied by*, *in addition to*, or *as well* do not change the number of the subject. If the subject is singular, the verb is too and vice versa.

  Examples: The Prime Minister together with his cabinet ministers visited the UN office.

  Sharon as well as Victoria attended the party.

  All your books, including mine, are on that shelf.

Having understood some basic rules of sentence formation, let us now look at different kinds of sentences.

Kinds of Sentences

There are three different kinds of sentences. These are simple sentences, complex sentences and compound sentences.

Simple Sentence is the basic form of sentence that contains only one clause. This sentence may be as short as a single-word sentence but it always contains a subject and a predicate.

Examples: Jump!

Jump on the floor.

Jump on the floor immediately.

There is a big fire on the top floor and unless we all jump down immediately we will all get burnt.

Looking at these examples, we notice that a simple sentence may be either short or at times even long, like the last sentence.

Simple sentences are used most commonly and extensively in spoken English. However, they may also be used in written English to draw the reader's attention to something particular.

Compound Sentence consists of two or more independent clauses joined together by a coordinating conjunction such as *or*, *and* or *but*.

Examples:

US is a prosperous country but it still has a number of poor people.

In this sentence, there are two independent clauses:

US is a prosperous country and *it still has a number of poor people*.

These clauses are joined together by the coordinating conjunction *but*.

A compound sentence is often used to create a sense of balance or contrast between two or more equally important pieces of information.

Example:

Julia is good in sports, but *her brother, James is good in studies*.

Some times, two independent clauses may be joined together by a semi-colon instead of a coordinating conjunction.

Examples:

Mr. Abraham had a serious drinking problem; when sober, he could talk better than most of the people.

Complex Sentence: consists of one independent and at least one dependent clause. Unlike a compound sentence, complex sentence often contains clauses that are not equal.

Examples:

Although she was invited for a party, she did not want to go.

A complex sentence makes it clear which ideas are more important. Let us look at the above sentence again:

Although she was invited for a party, she did not want to go.

Here, the fact that she was invited for a party is less important than the fact that she did not want to go.

Apart from these three basic kinds of sentences, there are also mixed sentences. Some times, we might notice that a coordinating conjunction instead of joining two simple sentences, joins together one simple and a complex sentence or joins together two complex sentences, it is referred to as mixed sentence.

Examples:

The boss came in the morning, but he left for an urgent meeting before I could speak to him.

Having looked at the various kinds of sentences, we are now in a position to understand that not all sentences make a single point. For example, compound sentences, as we noted above, may offer several equally important pieces of information. However, most of the time, when we write or speak sentences, there is a specific point, which we wish to get across to the reader or the listener, as the case may be. While framing sentences, the point of emphasis should be placed either at the beginning or at the end of the sentence. These are referred to as positions of emphasis.

Sentence Classification on the Basis of Its Order

Depending on its position of emphasis, a sentence may be either a loose sentence or a periodic sentence.

Loose Sentence

If a long sentence is structured in a manner such that the point of emphasis is placed at the beginning of the sentence, it is known as a loose sentence.

Examples:

I am willing to pay marginally higher taxes for the privilege of

living in Australia, considering the facilities provided by the government: free healthcare, subsidised education for children and monetary support till a new job is found.

In this sentence, the main point that comes across is the fact that the speaker wishes to live in Australia and whatever follows is extra information to support and corroborate this fact.

Loose sentences, then, are most natural sentences for speakers of the English language. These are also often used quite extensively in written English. However, it is important to structure a loose sentence cautiously because some times, it is easy to lose control of such sentences and often the listener or the reader may at the end of the sentence be unable to comprehend what was the point or meaning of the sentence.

Periodic Sentence

If a long sentence is structured in a manner such that the point of emphasis is placed at the end of the sentence, it is known as a periodic sentence.

Examples:

Considering the facilities provided by the government: free healthcare, subsidised education for children and monetary support till a new job is found, **I am willing to pay marginally higher taxes for the privilege of living in Australia.**

In this sentence, the main point that the speaker wants to live in Australia is mentioned at the end of the sentence. While listening or reading this sentence from its beginning, we cannot make out what is the purpose of the free healthcare and subsidised education for children unless we have read the complete sentence. Periodic sentences have over the time become less popular in both written as well as spoken English. However, some times, their use in a speech or a piece of written work may be necessary to break the monotony of loose sentences and to focus attention on certain specific points.

Sentence Classification on the Basis of Its Purpose

There is another classification of sentences that is based on the purpose of the sentence, which a particular sentence is trying to convey. As per their purpose, sentences may be declarative, imperative, rhetorical, exclamatory or interrogative.

Declarative Sentences

A declarative sentence is used to state an argument or a fact without requiring any action or answer from the reader or the listener. These are the most commonly used sentences in English language. A full stop is used to punctuate such sentences.

Examples:

Paris is the capital of France.

The distinction between capitalism and socialism is clear.

She wanted to know which way will lead towards the girls hostel.

Imperative Sentences

An imperative sentence gives a direct command or order to a particular person/s. Such a sentence may be punctuated with either a full stop or an exclamation mark.

Examples:

Jump!

Please give me a glass of water.

Rhetorical Sentences

Some sentences contain rhetorical questions and are known as rhetorical sentences. The reader or the listener is not expected to answer such questions.

Example:

Why did colonisation take place? Some historians believe that the white man's burden was responsible for this widespread global phenomenon, while some others believe that...

If used properly and not excessively, such rhetorical questions can be used as a way to introduce new topics in a long speech or in a written text. Such questions may also serve the point of focusing the attention of the reader or the listener to a new subject.

Exclamatory Sentences

An exclamatory sentence is a more forceful variant of a declarative sentence marked with the end punctuation, the exclamation mark.

Examples:

This boy did it!

How beautiful the hills look from here!

Although exclamatory sentences are quite common in spoken English, they are used quite sparingly in formal written English.

Interrogative Sentences

An interrogative sentence asks a direct question and is punctuated with a question mark at the end of the sentence. An important distinction between interrogative and declarative sentences is that while the former asks a direct question and is punctuated with a question mark, the latter asks an indirect question and is punctuated with a full stop.

Examples:

Who has not finished his work?

Which road leads to the guesthouse?

Now, let us look at the following sentences:

Which road leads to the Statue of Liberty? (Interrogative Sentence)

She wanted to know which road led to the Statue of Liberty. (Declarative Sentence)

The interrogative sentence as we notice asks a direct question, whereas a declarative sentence asks an indirect question.

■

PART IV

EXPANDING VOCABULARY

Vocabulary may be understood as a set of words known to a person or the word bank a person has at his/her command. Vocabulary means a set of words that a person is likely to use or draw upon in order to construct sentences.

If we look at our use of words in everyday life, we would observe that while framing or constructing sentences in both written as well as spoken English, we constantly draw upon the words and phrases known to us and those that we are familiar with. We would definitely not pick up a dictionary or any similar resource in order to frame sentences that would most appropriately convey the meaning we wish to. Such an activity would not only be cumbersome, but also extremely impractical most of the time. The most useful words and phrases that we often use are those that form a part of our vocabulary.

Expanding or building one's vocabulary forms an integral part of learning any language and refining one's existing skills in that particular language. It is for the same reason that in school, children are constantly taught new words and familiarised with their usage. Similarly, many adults also find vocabulary building exercises and activities fun-filled and educational.

If we view our everyday life from a distance, we notice that every day we meet and come across people from different backgrounds and those who come from varied walks of life. In order to interact with all these people most aptly, we need to draw upon different levels of vocabulary that we may be familiar with. For communicating with a child or a layman, we need to use simple words that are easy for the listener to understand. On the other extreme, if we are communicating with colleagues or superiors in a work organisation, we may require words that are more advanced than the simple, basic words.

Thus, we notice how crucial is the need for having a wide word bank at our command. It helps us to communicate more effectively with people from diverse backgrounds and walks of life. The idea is to get across our meaning without sounding too simple or too complicated, as the situation may demand. The key lies in framing our sentences perfectly, so that while they sound beautifully worded, they should not appear too basic or much advanced. For this reason, it is important that we constantly improve and expand our existing vocabulary levels. Regular vocabulary building helps us not only to keep in touch with new words that we learn, but also enables us to learn new words and learn to master their usage.

Vocabulary building is not a difficult or an uphill task. It just requires a little practice and consideration. An easy way to expand vocabulary is to start reading material that appears a little difficult to understand. In order to understand what the writer is wanting to say in that work, you will definitely need to consult a dictionary and in this way you would be able to learn the meanings of words hitherto unknown to you. Once you are familiar with the meaning of a particular word, try to use it a couple of times, so that you become familiar with the word, its meaning and its usage. Even before you realise, you would have mastered the knowledge and the usage of that word and it would soon enough form a new addition to your existing vocabulary. In this section on improving and expanding vocabulary, we shall look at some simple ways that can help to build and enhance vocabulary.

■

Lesson 18

Expanding Vocabulary while Reading

The easiest way to build your vocabulary is to inculcate a reading habit and try to read works that appear a little more advanced than your existing understanding and knowledge of words.

Let us see how reading can help in vocabulary building. While reading, we come across several new words or phrases. Even though we may not consult a dictionary, by just following the context in which these words or phrases have been used, we might be able to understand what the writer is trying to say by using that particular word or set of words. In fact, while reading there are several clues provided to the reader that help him/her to understand the meaning of the word used. Some such clues are:

- Context Clues
- Definition or Paraphrase Clues
- Example Clues
- Comparison and Contrast Clues.

Let us now see how each of these clues help us to understand the meaning that the writer is trying to convey through the use of a particular word.

Context Clues

While reading, when you encounter an unfamiliar or a new word, try to look at the context in which the word has been used and try to make out an approximate meaning of the word and understand its usage in that particular context. The other words in the same sentence as well as the previous and the following sentences provide important clues that can help a reader to understand what a particular word means in that given context. Understanding the context, in which the writer has used a particular word, provides handy clues about the meaning and the usage of that word.

Some times, it may not be possible to consult a dictionary. In such cases, understanding the context can help to understand the meaning of the word. Frequently, a reader is quite likely to remember a particular word by remembering the context of its usage. In such cases, a reader's prior experience with the word enables him/her to remember the word and its meaning and usage.

Let us attempt to understand this with the help of some examples:

The nice lady <u>courteously</u> opened the door for us.

a) quickly

b) rudely

c) slowly

d) politely

In this sentence, by understanding the rest of the words, we are able to understand that *courteously* means politely.

The matter has been decided by mutual <u>accord</u>.

a) conflict

b) agreement

c) action

In this sentence also, the words provide a clue about the meaning of the word *accord*. It means *agreement*.

The effect of the scandal on the election was <u>inevitable</u>.

a) Sudden

b) Certain

c) uncertain

d) gradual

Here also, the context helps us to understand that the word *inevitable* means *certain*.

Definition or Paraphrase Clues

Some times, the writer in the text itself provides definition or paraphrasing clues. By rephrasing the word or defining it, the writer many times, provides important clues to the readers that help them to understand the word better. This is especially noticed in scientific writings.

Examples:

The scientific theory that provides an explanation and understanding of human development across various stages is known as the theory of evolution.

Hypertension is used to denote a medical condition in which a person records blood pressure readings higher than the normal levels.

In these sentences, a definition clue helps us to understand the meaning of the word *evolution* and *hypertension*. We know by following the definition clues that evolution means development spanning across various stages and hypertension means a condition of higher than normal blood pressure levels.

Example Clues

Many times, writers provide readers examples of unfamiliar words that enable the reader to understand the meaning of the word by picking up from the example clues provided. In order to pick such clues, it helps to be alert enough to recognise the introduction of a series, by use of words like: *such as, examples, like, for example, for instance,* etc.

Hypertension is a serious disease, such as heart attack, high cholesterol, osteoporosis and diabetes- that if uncontrolled can become a silent killer.

Looking at this sentence and by following the example clues given, we are able to understand that hypertension is a serious disease, just like heart attack, high cholesterol, etc. and must be controlled.

Comparison and Contrast Clues

Often a lot of clues are provided in writings that serve to compare or contrast given items. By following the contrast or comparison, we are often able to understand the meaning of the sentence. Contrast clues help us to identify different things or qualities and comparison clues help us to identify similar things or qualities.

Examples:

Though Mr. David was very philanthropic in lending his support for most charitable activities, this time he was surprisingly stingy and scant in terms of his assistance to support this cause.

Looking at this sentence, even though a reader may not be familiar with meaning of *philanthropic*, by following the contrast clues provided, a person may be able to understand that *philanthropic* means the opposite of scant and stingy, that is, generous and big-hearted.

Thus, we notice that by paying a little attention to the literature that we are reading, we may be able to pick important clues that the writer constantly provides to us during his/her writing. These clues are often indispensable to an accurate understanding of the words used and the context in which they are used.

Learning new words through reading is one of the simplest and easiest ways to expand vocabulary. This is an activity that we all can indulge in because, however busy we may be in our daily lives, it is never difficult to find some spare time to read a book or any material that interests us, even a newspaper can serve the purpose!

Reading helps to keep the mind occupied and takes it away from reality, some thing that we all so ardently desire at some point or the other. And, what a better way to learn as you read! Regular reading helps us to come across new words and phrases that we may have often heard before but may not be familiar with their meanings and usages. Following the context and other such vital clues provided can help us to expand our word bank and build our vocabulary.

■

LESSON 19

Diction and Catch Phrases

Diction

Diction is simply the choice of words used to convey a meaning. Different words may be used in different contexts, even though they may mean the same.

Examples: I need help.

Is there any assistance available?

A lot of relief work is going on for the victims of the Tsunami disaster.

In these sentences, the words *help, assistance* and *relief* all mean the same but are used in different contexts.

Most often, our choice of diction depends on the kind of audience or reader segment that we are targeting. If we are trying to get the meaning across to a child or a layman, we will use the first sentence. If we are communicating with a more mature or learned audience, we may wish to use the last sentence.

The idea is to get the meaning across to the listener and also word it appropriately. For this reason, the assistance of certain commonly used catch phrases and synonyms and antonyms comes handy. In this section, we look at some commonly used catch phrases and in the following section; we shall turn our attention towards learning synonyms, antonyms and homonyms.

Catch Phrases

Catch phrases are certain phrases that are used commonly in English language. Let us look at some such phrases and attempt to understand their usage.

Examples:

1) to add fuel to the fire: meaning to escalate further an already heightened matter.

   The minister's speech far from helping sort out matters only **added fuel to the fire**.

2) Key to the future: means the answer or the path to the future.

   The nuclear energy holds **the key to the future**.

3) To blow one's own trumpet: to indulge in self-praise.

   Only a vain fellow **blows his own trumpet**.

4) To cut a sorry figure: to present a sad image.

   The famous cricketer **cut a sorry figure** in the first match of the tournament.

5) To keep at an arm's length: to maintain distance.

   It is advisable to **keep** bad company **at an arm's length**.

6) To keep in the dark: not to inform fully and correctly.

   The bank officials kept the gullible customer **in the dark**.

7) In today's world: in the present-day circumstances or environment.

   Cellular devices are the latest craze **in today's world**.

8) To nip in the bud: to destroy in the beginning only.

   Nip the evil **in the bud** and do not nurture it.

9) An open secret: known information and a fact that is no longer a secret.

   The fact that Ms. Sam Thatcher will be the favourite candidate for the Presidential elections is **an open secret**.

10) First and foremost: first of all.

Our **first and foremost** duty towards our work is to be honest and sincere towards the organisation.

11) A man of letter: a learned and an educated man.

Kofi Annan, the former UN President is **a man of letters**.

12) By hook or by crook: some way or the other.

He wants to win the election **by hook or by crook**.

13) A bird in hand: something that is available.

Instead of chasing futile dreams, it is better to be contented with the **bird in one's hand.**

14) A maiden speech: the first ever speech.

He came across as a powerful orator in his **maiden speech** only.

Catch phrases serve embellishment purposes in language. They are commonly used to beautify speech or text. But they need to be used cautiously because a poor expression using such phrases may often convey a poor image of the speaker to his/her audiences. Therefore, it is important that while using such phrases, the grammar, rhythm, accent and expression of the language must all be perfect and meticulous.

The list of catch phrases in English language is huge and regular reading and practice can only help a person to master the knowledge and the exact usage of such phrases.

■

LESSON 20

Homonyms, Synonyms and Antonyms

Homonyms

A homonym is a word that is similar to another word in terms of its spelling or pronunciation or both.

Let us look at some examples of homonyms:

1) Aisle and isle

He will be walking down the aisle with his bride today.

This is a beautiful isle.

2) break and brake

I will break your neck if you trouble me.

The brake was pressed and the car came to an abrupt halt.

3) birth and berth

Her birth date is 12th June 2002.

He got the lower berth in the train.

4) blue and blew

I like your blue shirt.

The wind blew Sam's shirt.

5) cheque and check

She received a cheque pertaining to payment for the work done by her.

I will check if all is well and come back.

6) cite and site

The teacher will cite many examples in support of the topic.

This site is under construction.

7) course and coarse

Is vocabulary a part of your English course?

This material is very coarse.

8) die and dye

The law of nature is that we are born to die.

I want this fabric to be cast in red dye.

9) deer and dear

The deer is a beautiful animal.

Dear sir.

10) dairy and diary

Mr. Jones owns a dairy farm.

Jack bought a diary to record the numbers of his friends.

11) dose and doze

I forgot to take the evening dose of this medicine.

She likes to doze off in the afternoons.

12) fare and fair

How much is the fare?

We all went to see the Christmas fair.

She is so fair.

13) feet and feat

Her feet are dirty.

The juggler displayed many a feat.

14) gate and gait

The gate is closed.

The player ran through the entire match with remarkable gait.

15) heal and heel

You must see a doctor if you want this wound to heal.

We must give enough rest to our heels because they support the weight of our entire body.

16) here and hear

All the drinks that we have are displayed here.

Do you hear what I say?

17) hole and whole

The ants went through a small hole in the wall.

Now, the whole story began to unfold.

18) herd and heard

See that herd of cows.

Have you ever heard any one tell such confident lies?

19) hair and hare

I am losing a lot of hair these days.

He likes chasing the hare.

20) knew and new

I knew that he would not join us for lunch.

Is this a new watch that you are wearing?

21) lesson and lessen

Let us re-look at what we learnt in this lesson.

This medicine will help to lessen the pain.

22) meet and meat

You meet me whenever you get free.

She likes to eat red meat.

23) not and knot

I know not what has happened to her.

She will finally tie the knot with her childhood sweetheart.

24) now and know

I think now, you all know what happened.

25) naughty and knotty

Isabella is a naughty child.

This is a knotty affair.

26) our and hour

I think we should all stand together in this hour of need.

This is our house.

27) principle and principal

He is a man of principles.

This lady is the Principal of this school.

28) plane and plain

He is very fond of planes and wants to be a pilot when he grows up.

She looked very plain in her casual dress.

29) pour and pore

The rain started to pour.

Our body loses sweat through pores called sweat glands.

30) pray and prey

Let us pray to God and thank Him for the bounties He has bestowed upon us.

The deer fell prey to an aggressive tiger.

31) peace and piece

Let peace prevail.

Can you give me a piece of that cloth with blue stripes?

32) pain and pane

The little boy cried in pain.

These boys broke the windowpane while playing football.

33) price and prize

What is the price of this dress?

He received the Nobel Prize for his efforts towards promoting world peace.

34) peal and peel

I love the peal of the church bells as they ring.

Peel off that orange.

35) rain and reign

It looks likely to rain heavily.

The Queen's reign was a period of peace and prosperity for the kingdom.

36) route and root

Which route will you take to reach to school?

Do you notice the tiny roots of the plant?

37) road, rode and rowed

Where does this road lead?

She rode a brown mare.

We rowed the boat.

38) Right, rite and write

This is not quite right.

After the last rites were performed, the group dispersed.

I shall write every thing down.

39) roll and role

The teacher called out the roll.

Would you like to eat an egg roll?

What role does Will Smith play in this movie?

40) sale and sail

The year-end sale is on.

The ship set sail.

41) steel and steal

This is made of solid steel.

Be careful, unless some one will steal your belongings.

42) sea and see

Just see how beautiful the sea looks!

43) seen and scene

I have seen it all.

This is a beautiful scene.

44) sight and site

What a wonderful sight!

The Smiths are looking out for a site to construct their new home.

45) suit and soot

Does this plan suit you?

He was dressed in a navy blue suit.

The chimney is filled with black soot.

46) sole and soul

The sole of this shoe is worn out.

The Devil will take away your soul unless you stop invoking him time and again.

47) story and storey

I like the story of this movie.

Her apartment is on the seventh storey.

48) stationary and stationery

The sun is the stationary object in this universe.

We have sent the list of stationery items that we need.

49) sore and soar

He has a sore throat.

The eagle soars high in the sky.

50) sun and son

The earth revolves round the sun.

He is my son.

51) their and there

They have their house built on a hillock.

Look there.

52) throne and thrown

Prince Williams descended the throne of England.

Who has thrown this book here?

53) teem and team

The sea is teeming with aquatic life.

He is the latest addition to our basketball team.

54) vain and vein

We tried in vain to persuade her.

The blood flows through a network of veins in the human body.

55) waste and waist

You should not waste food.

I need to lose some weight from my waist.

56) weather and whether

The weather is very enjoyable.

She asked her brother whether or not he would like to come along.

57) wear and ware

What will you wear tonight?

He is an expert of the computer software.

58) weak and week

He has grown very weak.

There are fifty-two weeks in a year.

59) weigh and way

Weigh your words before you speak.

Which way leads to the riverside?

60) wine and vine

Have you tasted some of this fine imported wine?

We visited a vineyard and saw grapes hanging on the vines.

61) weight and wait

What is your weight now?

I think we should wait for him.

62) too, to and two.

You can come along too.

She waved to her parents.

You two are very troublesome.

Synonyms

Synonyms are different words that are similar and identical in their meanings and can be easily used interchangeably.

Let us look at some words, their meanings and their synonyms:

Word	Meaning	Synonym
1) abandon	to give up without intent ro reclaim	foresake, relinquish.
2) abrupt	hastened	sudden.
3) apology	to ask forgiveness	pardon, excuse.
4) barren	deficient in production	sterile, infertile.
5) benevolent	a gesture of large-heartedness	generous, charitable.
6) candid	straight forward and impartial	fair, honest, upright.

7) chaste	pure	virtuous, pure.
8) compete	strive to attain perfection or mastery	contend, contest.
9) complacent	feeling or displaying a sense of satisfaction and pleasure at one's achievements	self-satisfied, self-pleased, self-contented.
10) copious	abundant, enough	plentiful, adequate.
11) deduce	to draw a conclusion	conclude, infer.
12) deteriorate	to pass from a higher to a lower state or condition	decline, downfall, descend.
13) desolate	may be used to mean uninhabited may also be used to mean gloomy	vacant, empty gloomy.
14) devout	showing fervour in the practice of religion	holy, religious.
15) ecstasy	intense exaltation of mind and feelings	blessedness, felicity, blissfulness.
16) efficacy	power to produce a desired effect	effective, efficient.
17) egocentric	concerned with an individual person rather than society	individualistic, self-centred.
18) eternal	something that is endless	permanent, everlasting.
19) futile	devoid of results	useless, ineffetual.
20) fragile	liable to be	delicate, breakable.
21) forbearance	quality of being patient	patience, endurance
22) genuine	a gesture or feeling that is real	authentic, actual.
23) grandiose	grand	grand, ostentatious.
24) grim	foreboding inaction or appearance	foreboding, omnious.

25) headstrong	some one who is used to having his/her own way with things	obstinate, untameable.
26) heritage	something that one receives or is entitled to receive by succession	legacy, inheritance, heritage.
27) hypothetical	a situation that is assumed and not real	abstract, supposed.
28) ignoble	belonging to socially or economically inferior classes	common, inferior, lowborn.
29) immaculate	pure, untouched	chaste, impeccable.
30) impeccable	correct and beyond criticism	flawless, perfect, immaculate.
31) irrevocable	incapable of being revoked	irreversible, established.
32) jinx	something that is meant to bring bad luck	ill-fated, cursed.
33) journey	passage or passing from one place to another	expedition, sojourn.
34) knowled-geable	possessing great knowledge	wise, intelligible.
35) lacklustre	lacking in lustre or colour	dull, colourless
36) latent	not manifest	dormant.
37) liberal	marked by generousity and open-handedness	generous, bounteous, benevolent.
38) malicious	having or showing vicious and intense ill-will.	malignant, malevolent.
39) melancholy	expressing or suggesting sorrow	gloomy, mournful.
40) mediocre	nothing great or extraordinary	average, commonplace.

41) nefarious	wicked or evil in intentions	vicious, wicked.
42) negligent	failing to give proper attentionn or care	careless, neglectful, delinquent.
43) obscure	withdrawn from human activity	unclear, cloudy, shadowy.
44) obscene	marked by words such that are regarded vulgar in polite usage	offensive, crude, indecent, gross.
45) omnipotent	having virtually umlimited power or influence	all-powerful, almighty.
46) oblivion	state of forgetting or having forgotten	forgetfulness.
47) pacify	to allay anger or agitation	appease, conciliate.
48) palatable	pleasant to the sense of taste	mouth-watering
49) paragon	a person with extraordinary and unequalled excellence serving as an example for others	ideal, model.
50) proficient	having or manifesting knowledge and skill needed for a particular field	adept, skillful, experienced.
51) quack	some one or something that is pretensive	counterfeit, pretender.
52) quarrel-some	apt or disposed to quarrel	belligerent, antagonistic.
53) quick-witted	one who is sharp and intelligent	sharp, intelligent.
54) reliable	having qualities that merit trust	dependable, trustworthy.
55) renowned	some one or something that is famous	famous, acclaimed.
56) repungnant	so unlikeable as to arouse aversion	repellent, repulsive, obnoxious.

57) rustic	an inhabitant of a rural or remote area characterised by total lack of sophistication	countryman, rural
58) sabotage	deliberate effort to hinder or prevent a plan or an activity	subversion, wreckage.
59) sacrilege	defilement of what is considered sacred	irreverece, blasphemy.
60) sagacious	wise, intelligent	prudent, judicious, clever.
61) spurious	of doubtful authenticity	illegitimate, unauthentic.
62) taboo	social or moral restraint	prohibition, forbiddance.
63) tactful	marked by or exhibiting tact	tactical, diplomatic.
64) tranquil	something that is calm	peaceful, quiet.
65) transitory	something that is changeable	transitional, impermanent.
66) ulterior	lying behind what is manifest	buried, concealed, guarded.
67) unanimous	being of one mind or sharing the same opinion	consentaneous, harmonious.
68) urbane	cosmopolitan	suave, sophisticated.
69) vacillating	given to or manifesting unsteadiness	unsteady, unsettled, double-minded.
70) vagrant	a person who wanders at will or as a habit	vagabond, derelict.
71) vociferous	loud, noisy and insistent as to compel attention	loud-mouthed, blatant

72) wreck	destroy, disable	ruin, destroy, sabotage.
73) worsen	to become worse	deteriorate
74) wretched	miserable	miserable, pitiable.
75) yearn	to longingly wish for or look forward to something	long, covet, desire.
76) youthful	possessing or displaying qualities of youth	young.
77) zeal	strong fervour or spirit	passion, enthusiasm
78) zenith	top most position	apex, summit.

Antonyms

Antonyms are word pairs that are opposites in meanings. Thus, an antonym of a word can be used as its opposite.

Let us now look at some words and their antonyms:

Word	**Antonym**
1) abrupt	gradual
2) always	never
3) aggression	resistance
4) abundant	scarce
5) associate	alienate
6) barren	fertile, productive
7) benevolent	malevolent
8) busy	idle
9) bold	shy, timid
10) barbaric	cultivated
11) chaste	unchaste
12) competent	incompetent

13) copious	meager
14) cold	hot
15) corrupt	upright
16) deteriorate	ameliorate
17) devout	undevout
18) diffident	confident
19) damned	blessed
20) dangerous	safe, secure
21) efficacy	inefficacy
22) eternal	transient, temporary
23) egoistic	altruistic
24) easy	difficult
25) edible	inedible
26) futile	effective
27) fragile	durable
28) forbearance	vindictiveness
29) flawless	flawed
30) genuine	ingenuine
31) grief	joy
32) guilty	innocent
33) guileless	guileful
34) gain	loss
35) headstrong	docile, tameable
36) humane	inhumane
37) hypothetical	actual
38) hot	cold
39) ignoble	noble

40) immaculate	maculate, unchaste
41) interested	disinterested
42) impeccable	deficient, faulty
43) jeopardy	safety
44) join	disjoin
45) just	unjust
46) knowledgeable	ignorant
47) kind	unkind, cruel
48) lacklustre	lustrous
49) latent	active, dynamic
50) lenient	stern, strict
51) long	short
52) malicious	considerate, kindly
53) melancholy	cheerful, joyous
54) mediocre	extraordinary, exceptional
55) marketable	unmarketable
56) melodious	unmelodious, discordant
57) negligent	attentive
58) noisy	noiseless, quiet
59) noble	base, cheap
60) obscure	clear, luminous
61) oblique	straight
62) ornate	plain, unembellished
63) obscene	decent, decorous
64) omnipotent	powerless, impotent
65) oppose	support

66) pacify	arouse
67) pardon	punish
68) proficient	incompetent
69) perfect	imperfect
70) qualified	unqualified
71) quarrel	agree
72) quick-witted	slow-witted
73) reliable	unreliable
74) religious	irreligious
75) refuse	accept
76) repel	attract
77) reveal	conceal
78) scarcity	abundance
79) scrupulous	unscrupulous
80) secluded	public
81) surplus	shortage
82) survive	perish
83) superiority	inferiority
84) tactful	tactless, untactful
85) tranquil	agitated
86) transitory	permanent
87) tolerant	intolerant
88) trustworthy	untrustworthy
89) unsympathetic	sympathetic
90) unanimous	discordant
91) unambiguous	ambiguous
92) upright	crooked, devious

93) vacillating	certain, resolved
94) valuable	worthless
95) vociferous	reserved, close-lipped
96) worsen	better
97) worthy	worthless, unworthy
98) willing	unwilling
99) yearn	dread
100) youthful	aged, elderly

■

Lesson 21

Idioms and Proverbs

An idiom may be defined as a group or a combination of words that has a meaning different from the meaning of the individual words. It may be understood as a phrase that does not adhere to the set rules of grammar and meaning. Its meaning can differ according to the circumstances in which it is used.

Let us understand this more clearly with the help of an example:

The idiom **a bad apple** does not mean an apple that has become bad and rotten. Quite to the contrary, it means a person who is morally corrupt and bad and can taint the entire company.

Due to this difference in the literal and the actual meaning of an idiom, often people unfamiliar with idioms may tend to get confused when they encounter such idiomatic expressions. Thus, as learners of English language, it is important to be familiar with idioms so that one can understand the meaning of sentences that are formed using these expressions. Knowledge of the idioms can also help a person to become familiar so as to use and understand idomatic expressions in common usage. Just like an understanding and knowledge of catch phrases helps to speak a well-worded language, idioms also help in much the same manner.

Speech containing occasional use of idioms helps the speaker to come across as one who is well-versed with English language, an impression that almost every speaker of English language, or for that matter, any other language, so ardently wishes to convey.

Let us now look at some commonly used idioms:

1) Idiom: a bad apple

Meaning: a morally bad/corrupt person who makes the entire company bad/corrupt.

Example: The debasement of this group started some years ago with Jack, **a bad apple** and now the entire group is known for their notoriety.

2) Idiom: be a piece of cake

Meaning: something that is very easy

Example: How was your English test today?

It was **a piece of cake.**

3) Idiom: be all ears

Meaning: to be interested in what some one is saying or is about to say.

Example: When the Principal started her welcome address to parents of new students, the parents were **all ears**.

4) Idiom: at the eleventh hour

Meaning: at the last minute/moment

Example: The doctor was called for **at the eleventh hour**.

5) Idiom: be the apple of someone's eye

Meaning: to be much loved by some one.

Example: Her only grandchild, Mark is **the apple of her eyes**.

6) Idiom: badmouth

Meaning: to say bad and unpleasant things about someone.

Example: I don't understand why she is always **badmouthing** her parents.

7) Idiom: blind as a bat

Meaning: to be unable to see well or unable to see at all.

Example: Without her glasses, she is **blind as a bat**.

8) Idiom: backfire

Meaning: to produce an unexpected or an opposite result.

Example: The Headmaster's memo to the teachers about the terms of obtaining a leave **backfired** as the teachers did not take the proposal too well and went on an indefinite strike.

9) Idiom: beat around the bush

Meaning: to delay or avoid talking about something.

Example: Mother said to Julia, " Don't **beat around the bush**. Tell me exactly what are you trying to say?"

10) Idiom: bite off more than one can chew

Meaning: try to something that is difficult.

Example: I don't want to **bite off more than I can chew**. I will finish this project by the month-end and the next one will be completed next month.

11) Idiom: bookworm

Meaning: some one who loves and enjoys reading very much.

Example: He was a real **bookworm** when he was young.

12) Idiom: the bottom line

Meaning: the most important factor to be considered in a particular situation.

Example: The **bottom line** is that if we launch this product before our competitiors, we will have a huge first mover's advantage.

13) Idiom: to bring the house down

Meaning: to make the audience enjoy or laugh a lot while making a performance or a speech.

Example: With his witty remarks, he always **brings the house down**.

14) Idiom: be broke

Meaning: to be without money.

Example: Sorry, I cannot join you for dinner because I am completely **broke.**

15) Idiom: to bug some one

Meaning: to bother or irritate some one

Example: He is always **bugging** us with his silly, self-made jokes.

16) Idiom: butterflies in the stomach

Meaning: to be nervous before doing something important.

Example: Abraham always has **butterflies in his stomach** before any public performance.

17) Idiom: can't make head nor tail of something

Meaning: unable to understand.

Example: This lesson is so tough that I **can't make head nor tail of it**.

18) Idiom: catch some one's eye

Meaning: to attract some one and make him/her look at something.

Example: While driving down the highway, a road sign **caught my eye.**

19) Idiom: cold feet

Meaning: to suddenly become very nervous about something that you were doing or were about to do.

Example: It's normal for people to get **cold feet** before their wedding.

20) Idiom: cold turkey

Meaning: to quit a bad habit, such as smoking or drinking, etc.

Example: David was a chain smoker for over two decades; then he quit smoking **cold turkey** and never smoked ever again.

21) Idiom: cool as a cucumber

Meaning: to be calm and relaxed even in tough situations

Example: She remained **cool as a cucumber** even as the boss sacked her and asked her to leave at once.

22) Idiom: cook some one else's goose

Meaning: to get some one into trouble and at times prevent from suceeding.

Example: He told his boss that he was unwell, but his colleague **cooked his goose** when he was spotted at a party the same night.

23) Idiom: couch potato

Meaning: a person who spends most of his/her spare time sitting idle and watching television.

Example: After her exams got over, she became a complete **couch potato**.

24) Idiom: to be cut from the same cloth

Meaning: to act in a similar way.

Example: Even though Julia and Jane are sisters, yet they are not **cut out from the same cloth**. Each is very different from the other.

25) Idiom: To be down in the dumps

Meaning: to feel sad, depressed.

Example: Ever since he has failed his final exam, he is **down in the dumps**.

26) Idiom: Don't let grass grow under your feet

Meaning: not to waste time and do something at once.

Example: As soon as she finished her education, she started working at once. She is the kind of person who **doesn't let grass grow under her feet**.

27) Idiom: to drive some one up the wall

Meaning: (a) to annoy or irritate someone.

(b) to put some one in an extreme and an unpleasant situation.

Example: His constant volley of silly questions, one after another **drives me up the wall.**

28) Idiom: eat out

Meaning: to eat food outside, instead of eating it at home.

Example: She is so fond of the spicy food that she often **eats out**.

29) Idiom: to eat one's words

Meaning: to admit what one said was wrong.

Example: The teacher told George that he would not be able to get promoted to the next class, but watching him stand first in the class, she had **to eat her words.**

30) Idiom: easy as pie

Meaning: something that is easy and simple to do.

Example: Cooking can be **as easy as pie**, if you know your ingredients well.

31) Idiom: fall in love with some one or something

Meaning: to start loving someone or something.

Example: When I first visited the Disneyland, I completely **fell in love with the beautiful place.**

32) Idiom: to feel like a fish out of water

Meaning: to feel uncomfortable because you are in an unfamiliar situation.

Example: Chris is not used to attending parties because they make him feel **like fish out of water.**

33) Idiom: be fishy

Meaning: suspicious

Example: He was offered an excellent business opportunity but he felt that there was something **fishy** about it.

34) Idiom: food for thought

Meaning: ideas that make you think.

Example: Mr. Abraham's speeches always provide much **food for thought**.

35) Idiom: wake up on the wrong side of the bed

Meaning: to feel angry or annoyed.

Example: John is really sullen and annoyed today. Looks like he has **woken up on the wrong side of the bed.**

36) Idiom: get over something

Meaning: begin to feel better again after having an unpleasant experience or after being sick.

Examples: She is **getting over jaundice**. (getting over sickness)

She took a long time to **get over her grandmother's death**. (getting over an unpleasant experience)

37) Idiom: give some one a hand

Meaning: help some one when he/she is doing something difficult.

Example: Don't worry about the project. I will **give you a hand** and we shall finish it before the deadline.

38) Idiom: be glued to something

Meaning: cannot stop watching or looking at something.

Example: When the news of the President's sudden demise in an air crash flashed, the entire nation **was glued to the television** and radio sets.

39) Idiom: go nuts

Meaning: become excited or get angry.

Examples: The spectators **went nuts** when they saw the

Australian cricket team hitting out at every ball the opponent team balled. (used to mean excited)

The teacher will **go nuts** if she sees what mess we have created. (used to mean angry)

40) Idiom: great minds think alike

Meaning: used as a humorous expression to indicate that you and some one else are thinking on similar lines or thinking about the same thing.

Example: Jane says to Henry, "I am going tonight to watch "Romeo and Juliet"."

Henry says to Jane, "Oh yeah! Even I am going for it."

Jane says, "**Great minds think alike**."

41) Idiom: grab a bite

Meaning: grab and eat food quickly.

Example: Work will never stop. You have to find time **to grab a bite**.

42) Idiom: hatrick

Meaning: used mainly in sports to denote a succession of three wins or accomplishments.

Example: Maradonna has already scored two goals. We are hoping that he gets a **hatrick**.

43) Idiom: a hand-me-down

Meaning: a cloth piece that has been handed down because its former wearer has outgrown it.

Example: As a child, he always wore his elder brother's **hand-me-downs**.

44) Idiom: heart sinks

Meaning: feel disappointed and hopeless.

Example: Her **heart sank** as she did not see her name in the list of the students who had been promoted to the next class.

45) Idiom: hit the books

Meaning: study very hard.

Example: The teacher said to the students, " The exams are just round the corner and you all must start **hitting the books** if you want to get promoted to the next class."

46) Idiom: Hold one's horses

Meaning: be patient and careful.

Example: **Hold your horses.** You might be able to find the same dress at the next store at a bargain.

47) Idiom: hit the ceiling/roof

Meaning: be very angry.

Example: Mother will **hit the roof** when she learns that I have failed in my exam.

48) Idiom: holy cow

Meaning: used as an expression of surprise.

Example: **Holy Cow**! How did she clear such a difficult exam?

49) Idiom: be in a pickle

Meaning: to be in a difficult situation.

Example: Sam **was in a pickle** when he discovered that he was not carrying his wallet and did not know what to say to the restaurant authorities in front of his girlfriend.

50) Idiom: be in the same boat

Meaning: to be in the same situation or the same problem as as someone else.

Example: No one has enough money to eat out tonight. We're all **in the same boat.**

51) Idiom: it's easier said than done

Meaning: easy to suggest or say than to actually do it.

Example: A said to B: "Why don't you forgive him for all his mistakes."

B said, " **It is easier said than done**."

52) Idiom: be in hot water

Meaning: to be in trouble or a troublesome situation

Example: I have **been in hot water** with my boss. I think he will fire me any day.

53) Idiom: it's about time

Meaning: something that has not yet happened should have been happened or something should have happened earlier than it actually happened.

Example: **It's about time** that you two get married. You have been seeing each other for as long as I can remember.

54) Idiom: Kill time

Meaning: to do something to keep yourself occupied, while waiting for something to happen.

Example: We **killed time** playing speller till the movie started.

55) Idiom: to know by heart

Meaning: to know something perfectly and completely.

Example: If you have any doubts, you can ask Smith because he **knows** the entire syllabus **by heart**.

56) Idiom: to keep an eye on something/someone

Meaning: to watch someone carefully to ensure that everything is all right.

Example: He is very naughty and may break glass items just for fun. You must **keep an eye on him**.

57) Idiom: the last/final straw

Meaning: the last event in a series of unpleasant events that makes a person accept the situation no longer.

Example: The poor economy and the rising inflation were

bad enough, but the people's revolt against the government was **the last straw** that brought an end to the dictatorial rule.

58) Idiom: let someone know

Meaning: tell some information to some one.

Example: If there is anything I can do to help you, please **let me know**.

59) Idiom: be like taking candy from a baby

Meaning: something that is easy to do.

Example: Convincing him to participate in the play was **like taking candy from a baby.**

60) Idiom: low-key

Meaning: a quite and a small-scale affair, not attracting much attention.

Example: Samantha and David want to keep their wedding a **low-key** affair but the reception will be elaborate and lavish.

61) Idiom: to make both ends meet

Meaning: to have or earn money enough just to live and meet the basic necessities.

Example: Pakistan is a poor country, where many people are struggling **to make both ends meet.**

62) Idiom: feel/look like a million dollars

Meaning: feel very happy or look attractive.

Example: Belinda **looked like a million dollars** yesterday in her lovely pink silk gown embroidered with pearls.

63) Idiom: not hold water

Meaning: something that does not seem reasonable or correct.

Example: The government's justification for going ahead with the nuclear pact with US **does not hold water**.

64) Idiom: be on the tip of someone's tongue

Meaning: unable to remember a thing or a word although you know it and know that you will remember it soon enough.

Example: His name was **on the tip of my tongue** and now I cannot seem to recall it.

65) Idiom: Once in a blue moon

Meaning: a rare event or occurrence

Example: How often do you go out?

Oh! **Only once in a blue moon.**

66) Idiom: out of the blue

Meaning: suddenly and unexpectedly

Example: Last evening, **out of the blue**, Smith announced that he had found a better job and will be joining the new company from Thursday.

67) Idiom: be over hill

Meaning: to be old to do something.

Example: At the age of thirty, I feel **over the hill** to engage in such childish pursuits.

68) Idiom: out of the frying pan and into the fire

Meaning: to get out of a difficult situation only to get into a worse situation.

Example: The thief while getting out of the house thought he had been spotted by the owner but fortunately enough was wrong since the owner did not notice him at all. No sooner had he heaved a sigh of relief than he was caught running by the guard on duty. **Out of the frying pan into the fire**.

69) Idiom: pop the question

Meaning: to ask someone to marry you.

Example: Jack has been seeing his girlfriend for five years

but still he has not mustered enough courage **to pop her the question**.

70) Idiom: pull someone's leg

Meaning: to tease someone.

Example: Since Stephen gets irritated very soon, we all love **to pull his leg**.

71) Idiom: to put all your eggs in one basket

Meaning: to depend totally on one person or a particular course of action.

Example: Financial experts believe that in order to minimise risks, it is wise to diversify your investments and not **to put all your eggs in one basket**.

72) Idiom: put yourself in someone's shoes

Meaning: to understand the situation that someone else is encountered with.

Example: Why don't you **put yourself in my shoes** and tell me what you would have done if you were in my position?

73) Idiom: read between the lines

Meaning: to guess someone else's thoughts, intentions or feelings from what you hear or read.

Example: He tried to be cheerful like always, but his mother was able **to read between the lines** and see that something serious was upsetting him.

74) Idiom: rain cats and dogs

Meaning: to rain very heavily.

Example: It was **raining cats and dogs** but we still did not cancel our travel plans.

75) Idiom: ring a bell

Meaaning: something that has been heard before or something that reminds one of something.

Example: Sorry, the name Joseph does not **ring a bell**.

76) Idiom: race against time/clock

Meaning: work very hard to finish something before the deadline.

Example: We studied eighteen hours a day, a **race against time**, in order to crack our Management exams.

77) Idiom: shake a leg

Meaning: hurry or do something now.

Example: We better **shake a leg** or else we will miss our last train also.

78) Idiom: see the light

Meaning: understand or believe something that you did not before.

Example: The people's rebellion against the court's judgement made the government **see the light** and re-open the case for fresh investigation.

79) Idiom: so far so good

Meaning: things have been going well so far.

Example: How is your new job going?

So far so good.

80) Idiom: be sold out

Meaning: nothing is left to sell.

Example: The show tickets have all **been sold out**.

81) Idiom: speak of the devil

Meaning: when someone you have been talking about enters the room suddenly and unexpectedly.

Example: How has Jeniffer been doing?

Oh! **Speak of the devil** and there she comes.

82) Idiom: surf the net/web/internet

Meaning: use the computer to look up at a number of websites.

Example: He often **surfs the web** to kill time.

83) Idiom: take a leaf out of someone's book

Meaning: to do something as someone else does it in order to be as successful as that person.

Example: It is high time that you **take a leaf out of Jack's book** and start preparing for your final exams if you do not wish to remain in the same class.

84) Idiom: to take it easy

Meaning: to relax.

Example: You have just recovered from typhoid. You must **take it easy** or else there may be a relapse.

85) Idiom: take to something like duck to water

Meaning: to learn how to do something very easily, quickly and well when doing it for the first time, especially because of the person's natural ability.

Example: How are Roger's swimming classes going on?

On! Great. He has taken to swimming **like duck to water**.

86) Idiom: that makes two of us

Meaning: I agree with you

Example: I don't understand what the teacher is talking about.

Yeah, **that makes two of us**.

87) Idiom: time will tell

Meaning: something will be clear in the future, time will tell whether it was good or bad.

Example: They have selected an Australian coach to train the Indian cricket team but only **time will tell** if this is a right decision or not.

88) Idiom: tip of the iceberg

Meaning: something that shows or suggests a larger problem.

Example: The terrorist attack in London today morning was just the **tip of the iceberg** because three more attacks followed in quick succession, all within the short span of one hour only.

89) Idiom: turn your back on someone

Meaning: (to) not help someone even though he/she may be needing your help desparately.

Example: This is a time when both of us should stand together and support each other. How can you **turn your back on me** in this hour of need?

90) Idiom: turn over a new leaf

Meaning: begin to do something in a new way, forgetting past errors and mistakes.

Example: He was a chain smoker once but now he has **turned over a new leaf**.

91) Idiom: twenty-four seven

Meaning: twenty-four hours a day and seven days a week.

Example: This shopping mall is open **twenty-four seven**.

92) Idiom: to be under pressure

Meaning: to live, work or act in a way that makes you feel worrisome and anxious.

Example: In March this year, we will all **be under pressure** because not only will there be the year-end closing to cope with, but also the auditors will be busy looking up our financial records at that time.

93) Idiom: be up in the air

Meaning: something that is not yet decided.

Example: Jack and Jane are getting married in early January

next year but the venue for their wedding is still **up in the air**.

94) Idiom: be up and running

Meaning: be working well and hard.

Example: Stephen had barely recovered from flu that he was soon enough **up and running.**

95) Idiom: to wear one's heart on one's sleeve

Meaning: display emotions or feelings publicly.

Example: It looks indecent when often young people can be spotted **wearing their heart on their sleeve.**

96) Idiom: when it rains it pours

Meaning: when one thing goes wrong many other things also go wrong.

Example: You wouldn't believe what happened yesterday. My computer crashed, my work that was saved on my desktop was unrecoverable and had to be re-done from the beginning. Worst of all, in order to finish the work, I could not sleep at night and missed the last bus to college today morning. It is rightly said, **when it rains it pours.**

97) Idiom: you can say that again

Meaning: I agree with you.

Example: Son: Dad, I have got bored watching this movie again and again.

Dad: **You can say that again**. I am going tomorrow to get new movies for you.

Proverbs

A proverb is a simple saying that is known popularly and is often repeated. Proverbs usually express truth, based on practical experience or common sense. The proverbs commonly used in English language have been borrowed mainly from the Bible and Latin.

As proverbs are short sayings, they are easy to remember and recall when required. They are old, familiar sayings that often offer advice. Much like idioms and phrases, proverbs too help to enrich our language, both verbal and written.

Let us now look at some commonly used proverbs in English.

1) beauty is the eyes of the beholder.

   This proverb is used to say that different persons have different opinions about what is beautiful and valuable.

   Example: Many people hated Rushdie's *Satanic Verses* for what they believed to be its anti-Islamic content. But **beauty is in the eyes of the beholder** for there were many others who quite liked the work.

2) better safe than sorry

   This proverb means that it is better to take some more time, effort and precaution, rather than to rush into something or take risks.

   Example: I drive very slowly because I feel it is **better safe than sorry**.

3) the best advice is found on the pillow

   If you cannot find a solution to a problem, instead of wasting time thinking about a possible solution, it is better to take a good night's sleep, for the answer may be found the next day.

   Example: Mother told John, "Don't worry about this thing too much now. Just go to sleep because often **the best advice is found on the pillow**.

4) the bigger, the better.

   This means that if something is bigger than the others, it is better than them.

   Example: He wanted a luxury car and bought a Mercedes. It ranks foremost in terms of luxury, comfort and is a class apart from all other cars. **The bigger, the better**.

5) a bird in hand is worth two in the bush.

This proverb is used to mean that whatever you have in hand or whatever is available is better than what is not. Wisdom lies in accepting what is available, rather than to run after what is not.

Example: If I was in your place, I would have accepted this business offer. It may not be what I am looking for, but **a bird in hand is worth two in the bush.**

6) birds of a feather flock together.

People who are very similar to each other, tend to gather together and become friends.

Example: Sara is very pious and goes to the church every Sunday. Her dear friend, Sam is also like her.

Well, **birds of a feather flock together**. This might be the reason that they are such bosom friends.

7) curiosity killed the cat

This proverb is used to mean that people who are too interested in things that they should not be interested in, could be in a dangerous situation or position.

Example: Yesterday, at around midnight, I heard a scary voice from the empty house next door. I wanted to see if all was well, but my husband stopped me. He said, " You know **curiosity killed the cat**. There might be some problem and you would be safer here than outside."

8) don't count your chickens before they hatch.

This is used to mean that you should not plan something that depends on a good thing that is likely to occur in future. It is better to wait for the events to unfold on their own.

Example: I plan to buy some dresses for my parents and my brother, when I get my first salary the next month.

Sounds great, but **don't count your chickens before they hatch**.

9) don't cross your bridges before you get to them.

Not to worry about something, until it actually happens.

Example: The proposal looks great, but what if the boss turns it down?

We'll see what happens. **Don't cross your bridges before you get to them**.

10) good things come in small packages.

The proverb is used to mean that the size of things does not determine their quality. There are often many good-quality, small things that are better than their bigger counterparts.

Example: Why did you decide to buy your wedding dress from such a small store? There are many others that sell much stylish and more trendy dresses.

I am aware that some other stores sell much trendy dresses, but this store sells only quality products and their products are really one of their kind. You see, **good things come in small packages.**

11) the early bird catches the worm.

This is used to tell a person to act early in order to be successful.

Example: Although there are still six months before your wedding date, you must start looking out for your wedding ring right now because you may be able to pick a good piece at a reasonable price, without hurrying too much. **The early bird catches the worm**.

12) the grass is always greener on the other side of the fence.

This means that things and situations of other people always appear more lucrative than our own.

Example: Jack said to John, " Stephen's wife is so talented and beautiful. I wish my wife was also like her."

John said to Jack, " Your wife too is very talented and pretty.

Its just that **the grass is always greener on the other side of the fence.**"

13) it's no use crying over spilled milk.

Whatever has been done, cannot be undone and it does no good to waste time repenting over what is lost.

Example: Mother said, " It's **no use crying over spilled milk** now. If you had listened to me and not wasted your precious time, you would have cleared this entrance exam. But, now, you can try again the next time."

14) home is where the heart is.

It means that if you are in the company of the person you love the most or if you are in a place that you love, you are at comfort, at home.

Example: Don't worry too much about where you will live the next month, when you get the new job. **Home is where the heart is**.

15) necessity is the mother of invention.

If someone really needs something or has a problem, he/she will find a way to do it or solve it.

Example: If we look at the history of scientific innovations, we find that **necessity is the mother of invention.**

16) money doesn't grow on trees.

It means that money should not be wasted or that there is not enough money to buy something.

Example: We desparately need to buy a new house, but we cannot afford it now. **Money doesn't grow on tress.**

17) opposites attract.

This is used to mean that people tend to be attracted to those who are not like them in terms of likes, dislikes, appearances, etc.

Example: Jack and Jane have nothing in common. While

Jane is an extrovert and loves to socialise and frequents parties, her husband, Jack is an introvert who hates socialising and does not like partying.

Well, that's reason they are together. As they say, **opposites attract.**

18) an ounce of prevention is better than a pound of cure.

It is easier to prevent a problem rather than to spend time later to cure it or to set it right.

Example: The software enginner suggested that we get the anti-virus programme installed on our PCs. **An ounce of prevention is better than a pound of cure.**

19) a picture is worth a thousand words.

A picture can provide as much information as can be provided by a text filled with several words.

Example: Foreign toursits can often be spotted trying to discover routes by following maps that can lead them to their destinations in alien lands. It is rightly said, **a picture is worth a thousand words.**

20) the pen is mightier than the sword.

It is used to mean that you can achieve your purpose better by means of communication with words rather than resorting to violence.

Example: Failing to get the government pay heed to his complaint, David Jones decided to write an article about the entire episode and have it published in a newspaper because he had come to believe that **the pen is mightier than the sword.**

21) a stitch in time saves nine.

It is better to spend some time to deal with problems or act now rather than wait. Waiting may often make things more difficult to deal with.

Example: Mother says it is better and easier to deal with problems as they arise instead of postponing them for future because **a stitch in time saves nine**.

22) silence is golden.

In difficult situations, it is much better to be silent and quiet.

Example: When all the other people were screaming and getting angry at the government's inability to take any concrete action in this matter, Mr. Smith stood quiet and did not say a thing. They say rightly, **silence is golden** for his silence helped to resolve his problem, while the others are still waiting for an answer to their queries and complaints.

23) safety lies in the middle course.

When faced with two extreme and difficult situations, it helps to adopt a middle path.

Example: Since both the supporters as well as opposers to the government's foreign disinvestment policy were unwilling to budge from their repective stands, the government adopted a mid-way and the problem was solved. They say rightly, **safety lies in the middle course.**

24) too many cooks spoil the broth.

If too many people do the same thing, it will not be done properly.

Example: The boss always appointed two officers to take charge of different matters. She did not like to involve many because she believed that **too many cooks spoil the broth.**

25) time flies.

The expression is used to denote that minutes, hours, days and even years pass by quickly, without us realising that so much time has passed.

Example: Does it look like we have known each other for eleven years now?

No, it just seems like yesterday. See how **time flies**.

26) there's no place like home.

Home is a special place and nothing can replace it.

Example: No matter where you go, **there's no place like home**.

27) variety is the spice of life.

If you do different things and meet different people, life becomes interesting.

Example: He loves meeting people and making new friends. The proverb, **variety is the spice of life** holds true for him.

28) you can't take it with you when you die.

This is used to mean that when you die, you leave behind all your earthly possessions, valuables, money, etc.

Example: I don't understand that even in your old age, why are you so busy collecting and saving things? **You can't take it with you when you die**.

29) you can lead a horse to water, but you can't make it drink.

You can give someone an opportunity but you cannot make that person accept that opportunity.

Example: Father says to mother, "Joseph doesn't seem to understand how important it is to find a stable job. He seems to be changing jobs like clothes. I have tried to counsel him, but all to no avail."

Mother to father, " Don't worry he will understand it some day. **You can lead a horse to water, but you can't make it drink."**

30) you can't judge a book by its cover.

Exterior looks or appearances cannot be used to judge what a person or a thing actually is.

Example: This car looks great and I will buy it when it is launched next month.

You can't judge a book by its cover. I think you should wait for some time after its launch before you actually buy it.

The list of idioms and proverbs used in English language is enormous and it is not possible to incorporate all of them in any one book. The examples discussed here are aimed at only familiarising you with some of those expressions that are used most commonly and the ones that we encounter in our daily lives.

Familiarity with idioms and proverbs will help you to identify these expressions in everyday usage. Regular practice, an alert eye and an attentive ear will help you to pick many more similar expressions that you might come across while conversing with other people or reading books, etc.

Start using these expressions that you get to learn and even before you realise, you would have mastered their use and would have become familiar with most of such expressions that form the English vocabulary. Needless to mention, that knowledge of these expressions will help to enrich your vocabulary and help you to get across to others as a learned and an educated person.

■

CONCLUSION

This brings us to the end of this book and also completes the first stage of learning, that is understanding and familiarity with concepts of English pronunciation, grammar and vocabulary. By now, you would have become familiar with all the essential concepts of English language. Having finished reading this book and having grasped the concepts underlined here is just half the battle won. There still a lot to do and learn.

This brings us to the next stage of learning, that is gaining fluency and mastering the concepts learnt.

Whenever we learn any new language, the only way to improve is practice, practice and only practice. Reading any book can no doubt help us to understand essential concepts, but the only way that we can remember the concepts learnt is by way of practice.

Let us look at some interesting ways that can help you to keep in touch with whatever has been learnt and at the same time also help in constantly improving the level of knowledge gained.

Chat your way to Better English

One of the easiest ways to keep in touch with whatever has been learnt is to incorporate the same in your daily lives and speech. As you interact and communicate with others, it helps you to utilise the concepts learned theroretically and put them into action.

Chatting with others also helps to acquaint us with words, phrases, etc. that are unknown to us. By observing others use those words, we can understand the context in which these words were used and attempt to use them in a similar context ourselves.

Chatting will help to erode any hesitation or lack of confidence that you may be experiencing. Sometimes you may be pleasantly surprised by your grammatically accurate and perfect English. There are instances such as this, that will help to do away with any shyness or holding back where English speaking is concerned. It will help to boost your confidence and make you feel that even you can speak English beautifully and well just as any native English speaker.

Improving Through Reading

Another very simple way is to keep in constant contact with the concepts learned through reading. Reading newspapers and books cannot only help to utilise some spare time that you may often have at hand, it can also be educative and informative. While reading, you may often encounter new words, phrases, idioms, etc. and learn those hitherto unknown. Thus reading will help not only to keep in touch with whatever has been learned, but will also help to improve the existing level of your learning.

Online Puzzles and Exercises

The Internet has a wealth of resources that can help you to improve and learn. Many interesting word games, puzzles and grammar exercises are available online that can serve as an interactive approach to practising English grammar and vocabulary. There is an exhaustive variety of exercises, puzzles and quizzes and you can pick those most appropriate according to your level of learning. Most of these exercises also provide answers and explanations that can help you to understand and learn new concepts.

Watching English Channels

You can even learn as you watch television or listen to radio. Watching English channels on television and listening to English radio stations can help to improve English listening skills.

Often native English speakers speak very fast and sometimes

non-native speakers may find understanding their speech a little problematic. In such cases, watching and listening to English channels on television and radio and watching English movies can be very helpful. This will not only help to sharpen listening skills, but can also help you to pick up many new words.

Thus, we see that apart from reading English books, which can be monotonus if done all the time, there are many new and more interesting ways that can help us to perfect our understanding and knowledge of English and constantly improve our English-speaking skills, so that even we can become a fluent speaker of a beautifully worded and grammatically correct English.

■

Other Books on
WORD POWER SERIES

1. Idiomatic English (How to Write & Speak It) **(New)**
2. School Essays, Letters, Applications, Paragraphs, and Stories For Higher Secondary Students **(New)**
3. Effective English Comprehention Read Fast, Understand Better! **(New)**
4. Latest Essays for College & Competitive Examinations **(New)**
5. Dictionary of New Words **(New)**
6. Art of English Conversation Speak English Fluently **(New)**
7. Teach Yourself English Grammar & Composition **(New)**
8. Common & Uncommon Proverbs **(New)**
9. Effective Editing Help Yourself in Becoming a Good Editor **(New)**
10. Effective English A Boon for Learners **(New)**
11. Essays for Primary Classes
12. Essays for Junior Classes
13. Essays for Senior Classes
14. Dictionary of Synonyms and Antonyms
15. Dictionary of Idioms and Phrases
16. Common Phrases
17. How to Write & Speak Correct English
18. Meaningful Quotes
19. Punctuation Book
20. Top School Essays
21. How to Write Business Letters with CD
22. Everyday Grammar
23. Everyday Conversation
24. Letters for All Occasions
25. School Essays & Letters for Juniors
26. Common Mistakes in English
27. The Power of Writing
28. Learn English in 21 Lessons
29. First English Dictionary
30. Boost Your Spelling Power

31. Self-Help to English Conversation
32. The Art of Effective Communication
33. A Book of Proverbs & Quotations
34. Word Power Made Easy
35. English Grammar Easier Way
36. General English for Competitive Examinations
37. Spoken English
38. School Essays, Letters Writing and Phrases
39. How to Write & Speak Better English
40. Quote Unquote (A Handbook of Famous Quotations)
41. Improve Your Vocabulary
42. Common Errors in English
43. The Art of Effective Letter Writing
44. Synonyms & Antonyms
45. Idioms
46. Business Letters

Lotus PRESS